Stitch drawing – the act of using a needle and thread to draw with – is a method of textile artistry quickly growing in popularity. In this book, figurative stitch expert Rosie James reveals the huge creative scope these techniques offer. The first step is simply to pick up a pen and start drawing.

Beginning with exercises for drawing from observation, memory and photographs, as well as ideas for recording special events and gathering inspiration on the move, the book moves on to demonstrate how to get to grips with the sewing machine and transfer your drawings on to fabric, with step-by-step examples for getting started with your first stitch picture. Once you have mastered the basics there are plenty of exciting ideas for experimenting with unusual fabrics, different ways of using thread, incorporating blocks of colour and pattern, or combining with other techniques such as appliqué or screen-printing.

Showcasing a range of beautiful work from leading stitch artists, this book is as much a celebration of stitch drawing as it is a practical guide, and will open up the inspirational world of figurative stitch for both beginners and professionals.

Stitch Draw

Stitch Draw

Rosie James

BATSFORD

First published in the United Kingdom in 2014 by
Batsford
10 Southcombe Street
London W14 0RA

An imprint of Pavilion Books Group Ltd

ISBN: 9781849941570

A CIP catalogue record for this book is available from the British Library.

20 19 18 17 16 15 14
10 9 8 7 6 5 4 3 2 1

Reproduction by Mission, Hong Kong
Printed by Craft Print Ltd, Singapore

This book can be ordered direct from the publisher at the website:
www.anovabooks.com, or try your local bookshop.

Distributed in the United States and Canada by Sterling Publishing Co.,
387 Park Avenue South, New York, NY 10016, USA

Exhibition Row (page 1), detail
from *Ripley Wedding* (page 2)
and *City Streets* (below) by
Rosie James.

Contents

Introduction

Stitch drawing is the act of using a needle and thread to draw with, just as you might use a pencil or pen. In this book we are going to focus on using a sewing machine to 'draw', rather than stitching by hand.

Artists have been using thread to draw with for years. A good example of this is the Bayeux Tapestry, which dates from the eleventh century. It is interesting that stitch was used to make drawings of actual events and to tell a story, rather than paint on canvas or pencil on paper. Wall hangings were common at that time, but The Bayeux Tapestry seems to be the only surviving example of medieval narrative embroidery that we know of.

Since then embroidery as an art form has gone in and out of fashion. Today artists use all sorts of materials to create their work, and threads and fabrics are almost as common as paint or sculptors' materials.

When you draw with a pen or pencil, the instrument becomes an extension of your hand and you can respond to what you are seeing immediately. The sewing machine is a totally different beast, in that you cannot respond quite so immediately to what's in front of you, yet with a bit of practice, you can move the cloth and hoop fluidly and draw directly from life. However, most of the stitched drawings we will look at in this book will be drawn with pencil first and then transferred to the stitching surface.

Photography also plays a big part. I use it as a way of getting ideas and also for capturing moving images. We will be looking at how to draw from photographs as well as manipulating photographs on the computer.

Stitching made with a sewing machine lends itself to a certain kind of fluid line. As Paul Klee put it, 'Drawing is taking a line for a walk.' A sewing machine will follow a line continually for as long as you have your foot on the pedal. All you need to do is to guide that line in a particular direction to create a drawing in stitch. And you do not have to be an expert on a sewing machine in order to make drawings with it, as you will see.

> Detail of a life-size figure from *Crowd Cloud* (see page 72). Notice how the stitching takes 'a line for a walk', in a continuous, flowing movement.

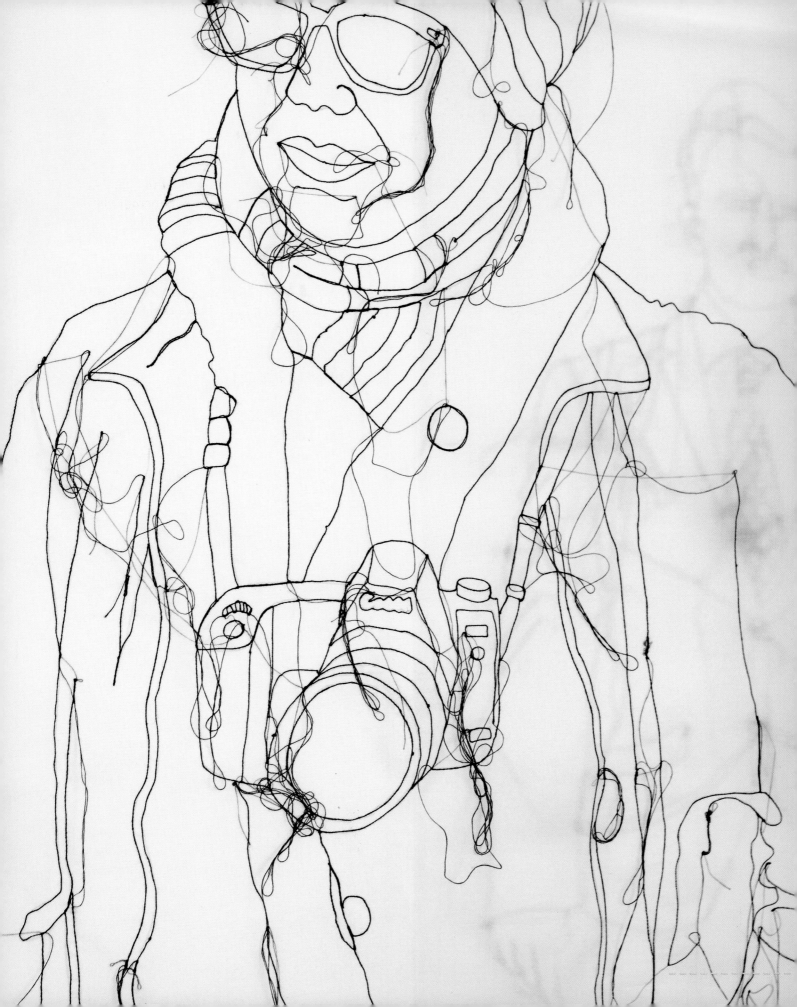

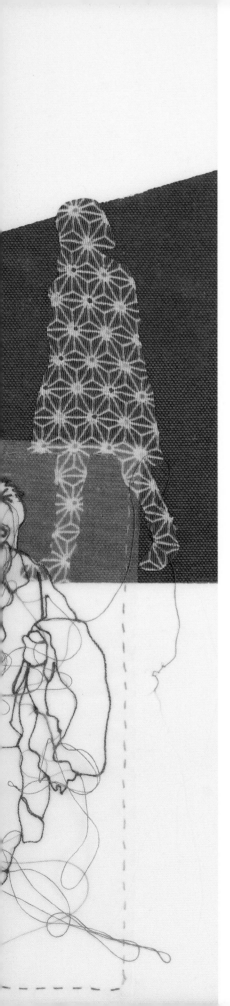

Drawing

Lets begin by drawing with a pen or pencil on paper. This will get you started and give you exciting drawings that can be developed into stitch.

Pencil and paper

In order to get really good at stitch drawing with a sewing machine, you need to start with the basics – drawing with pencil on paper – which allows you to draw more directly from what you see than you would if you attempted to stitch-draw straight off. These drawings can form the basis of your later stitched drawings. So let's start drawing.

Drawing is essentially all about looking. In order to create a good drawing, you need to look carefully at the object you are drawing. Spend more time looking at the object than at the paper you are drawing on.

So get yourself a piece of paper and something to lean on, or open a page in your sketchbook. Use a soft pencil that creates a nice dark line which doesn't smudge too easily – something like a 2B.

Flex your drawing muscles

Here are some exercises to try: just enjoy them and see what comes out. You can go on to interpret some of the results in stitch, as we shall see later.

Exercise 1: looking
Find an object you are really familiar with, such as a favourite shoe, old coat or a bag, as in this example. Put the object in front of you, then close your eyes and imagine the object in your mind's eye. Try to see its colour, its form, its texture and its scale. Then open your eyes. How does the object look? Try to spend two minutes (or longer) examining the object in great detail. This might seem like a long time, but don't cheat. Then close your eyes and imagine the object in your mind's eye again, this time in much greater detail.

> Study a familiar object then close your eyes. How much detail can you remember?

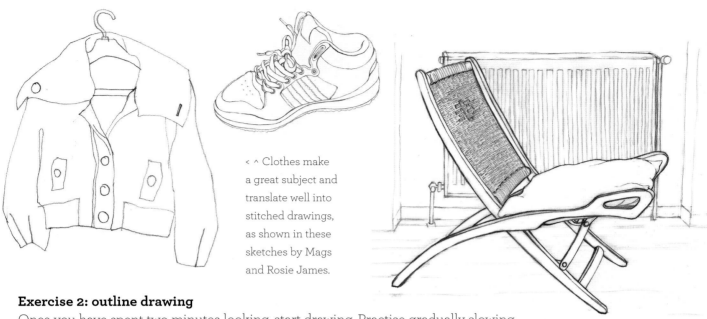

< ^ Clothes make a great subject and translate well into stitched drawings, as shown in these sketches by Mags and Rosie James.

Exercise 2: outline drawing

Once you have spent two minutes looking, start drawing. Practise gradually slowing down the speed at which your eyes travel over the object until it is painstakingly slow. Then pick up a pencil and start drawing at exactly the same speed, moving the pencil across the paper at the same speed as your eyes move over the object. Draw *only* the outline of the object; as your eyes move along an edge, so the pencil moves on the paper. Glance down at your drawing occasionally and then look back at the object. Now add some detail inside the outline, but not too much; keep the drawing simple and uncluttered. Outline drawing is also known as contour drawing.

^ ˅ Above is a drawing of a folding chair. Below left is the same subject but only the negative spaces are drawn.

Exercise 3: negative space

For this exercise, you are going to focus upon the space *around* an object rather than the object itself. This is called negative space. For instance if you were drawing the legs of a chair, you would focus on the space between the legs and draw that rather than drawing the chair legs, as shown left.

Once you have become used to seeing things in two ways (as solid objects, and as objects bound by negative space), make a drawing in which you draw the negative space around an object. Because the shapes of a negative space are less recognizable, you really have to look carefully to see them – you can't guess and draw what you think is there.

Use this technique whenever you are struggling with drawing an object. Switch your mind to seeing the negative space, and try drawing that instead.

Another way to identify negative spaces is to imagine that the object is surrounded by black space and draw the black shapes created by the object.

TIP: To help understand a negative space, make a viewfinder (a piece of card with a window cut into it of the same proportions as the drawing paper). Hold the viewfinder in front of your eyes to frame the object you are drawing. Use the frame of the viewfinder to create a boundary for the negative space.

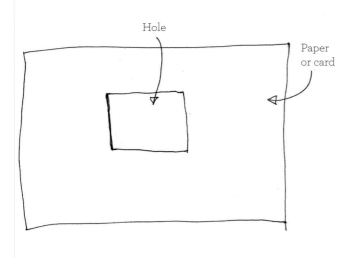

Hole

Paper or card

Exercise 4: isolating the essence

Draw the same object you drew before but only use ten lines. Then do another drawing using only eight, then six and then four lines. Is it still possible to tell what the object is?

˅ Draw your subject then draw it again using only ten lines. Can you draw it with even fewer lines?

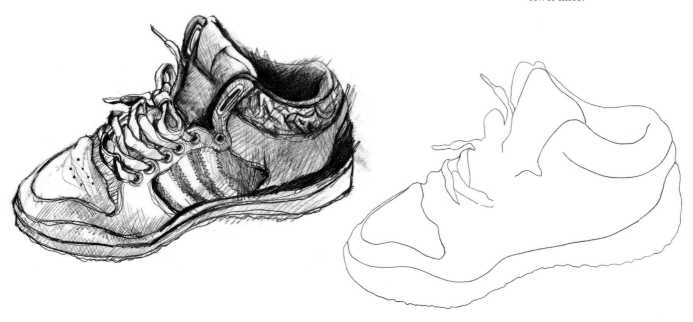

Exercise 5: time limit

Give yourself a strict time limit. Start with five minutes, and then make the time limit shorter and shorter until you are down to ten seconds. You will have to work very quickly and it will stop you worrying too much about what the drawing looks like. Set a timer for this exercise so you don't waste time checking the clock every few seconds.

Exercise 6: eyes shut

Draw an object with your eyes open, then repeat the process with your eyes shut (don't look at the paper at all). If you need to stop and start elsewhere, you have to guess where to start again. This will give a quite lively but distorted drawing. Now compare the results.

Then move on to something more complicated, such as a self-portrait. Stare at your face in a mirror for a good two minutes and then attempt to draw it with your eyes closed. Doing this 'blind' frees you up from having to make a drawing that looks like you and you may create something much more interesting.

˅ Draw with your eyes open first, as it allows you to really look at the object.

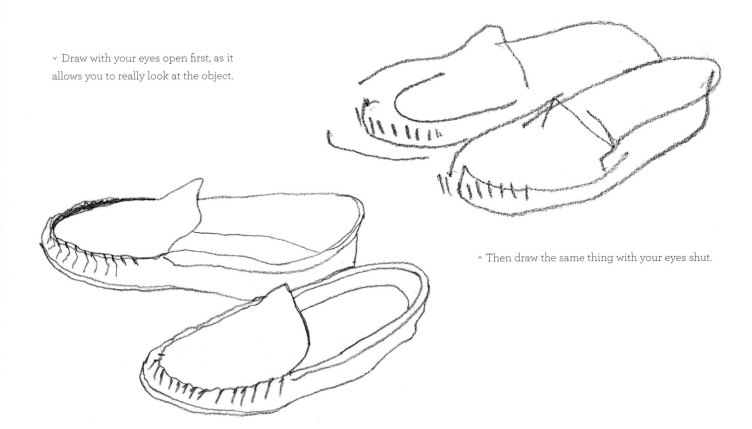

^ Then draw the same thing with your eyes shut.

Drawing figures

Figure drawing is a fascinating yet daunting proposition. We know what a person looks like and we want our drawing to look exactly like him or her: we want realism. Well, some of the best drawings of people are those that are less 'real'. So forget about trying to achieve a realistic representation and just have fun. Draw your best friend and make her look hideous – it's much more interesting!

Here are three methods to employ when drawing people: drawing from observation, drawing from imagination, and drawing from photographs. Try them all and then use the method that suits you best, or mix them all up and use together in one piece.

Drawing from observation

This is where you can use some of the things you learned in the drawing exercises earlier, but this time focused on people.

Posed models
This is the easiest place to start, because a model's brief is to keep still, which makes him or her much easier to draw. Ask a friend or family member to pose for you. She could sit, stand, lie down or adopt a fashion pose, for example. Look at paintings of people and also fashion magazines for ideas.

Make sure that the model can sustain a pose long enough for you to draw her. Start with quick poses of five minutes to get your drawing skills warmed up, and then ask her to pose for 30 minutes. Have a break and then get the model to adopt a one-hour pose.

Try contour drawing (just drawing outlines: see page 11) to start with, and then bring in some shading, but remember that this a drawing that you are going to stitch, so focus mainly on line.

^ Mags James made this quick drawing in her sketchbook, focusing on a simple line and working quickly so she didn't have time to worry too much about perfect proportions.

> Make a simple drawing of a face and add bits from your imagination – for example buildings or a rabbit.

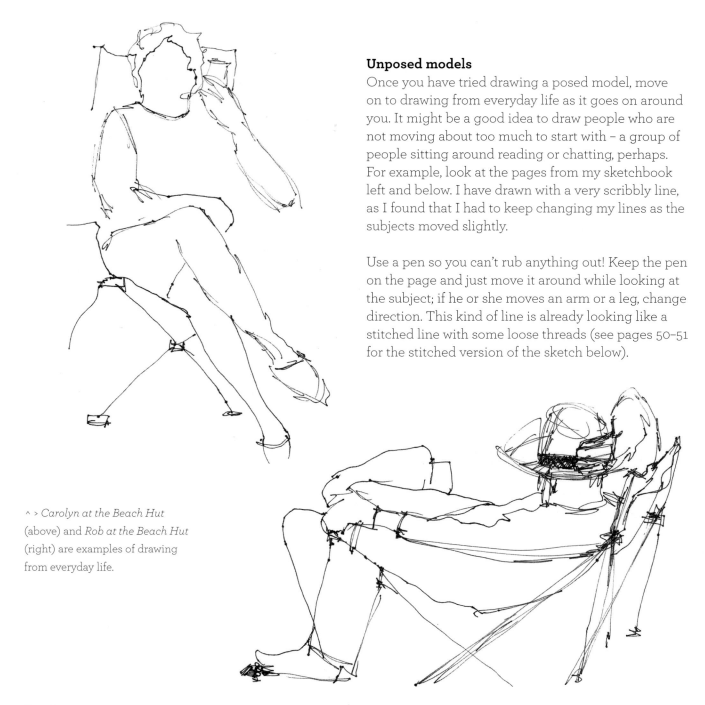

Unposed models

Once you have tried drawing a posed model, move on to drawing from everyday life as it goes on around you. It might be a good idea to draw people who are not moving about too much to start with – a group of people sitting around reading or chatting, perhaps. For example, look at the pages from my sketchbook left and below. I have drawn with a very scribbly line, as I found that I had to keep changing my lines as the subjects moved slightly.

Use a pen so you can't rub anything out! Keep the pen on the page and just move it around while looking at the subject; if he or she moves an arm or a leg, change direction. This kind of line is already looking like a stitched line with some loose threads (see pages 50–51 for the stitched version of the sketch below).

^ > *Carolyn at the Beach Hut* (above) and *Rob at the Beach Hut* (right) are examples of drawing from everyday life.

Setting

Consider the surroundings of your posed model and draw this instead of the person. Leave a blank shape where the person is. This is the same technique as negative space drawing (see page 11) and will give you a lovely silhouette surrounded by a detailed, interesting background. This lends itself to stitch and appliqué (see Appliqué, page 92).

Clothes

For me, this is the fun bit! Dress your posed model in something striking and dramatic, which has an interesting detail or shape. For example she could wear a large hat, a belted coat with lots of pockets, huge boots, or a voluminous skirt. If a garment involves lots of fabric and draping, it will be visually stimulating.

Drawing from imagination

Here are a few things you can try in order to draw a figure from your imagination. Have fun with this, as there is no real version you are trying to copy: the drawing can be whatever you want it to be.

Exercise 1: doodling
Start off by doodling and see what happens. You could maybe invent some weird creatures coming out of the shapes of your doodles.

> *Brushes Up The Teeth* by Mags James, from her sketchbook.

> *Agitated* by Mags James, from her sketchbook. Drawings that begin as doodles often include words or geometric shapes. This is fine. Allow the drawing to be what it wants to be.

Exercise 2: imaginary situations

Imagine yourself in a situation and make a drawing of it without looking in a mirror or posing or looking at photographs. You could be swimming, standing on your head, climbing a tree or reading a book.

Try to picture the scene in your head and draw that. Don't worry about getting it right. See what comes out, work quickly and do a few sketches in order to get the hang of it first.

Exercise 3: imaginary faces

Draw faces – lots of them. Vary the types of eyes, noses, lips, eyebrows, ears and hair. Start to be more fantastical – add weird elements and extensions; put them in the wrong place; be free.

> *Faces Mean It All* by Mags James, from her sketchbook. When drawing imaginary faces you can really let your creativity flow.

SPOTLIGHT: Rachel Coleman

Rachel's artwork uses simple, naive imagery to create multi-layered, embroidered textile pictures that explore personal anecdotes, memories and childhood narratives. She uses recycled fragments of vintage fabrics, machine-embroidered graphic lines, traditional embroidery techniques and reclaimed ephemera to evoke a sense of nostalgia. Rachel comments: 'It's the small, everyday things that I find most interesting, such as an object or a word or colour that reminds me of my childhood. I try to let my work develop organically so that I can retain the vibrancy of the moment I am trying to convey.'

Rachel's range of whimsical animal pieces has been lovingly created from the exploits of her menagerie of animals, including guinea pigs and rabbits.

> *Leaping Rabbit* by Rachel Coleman. A lively mixed-media piece using black thread, mixed fabrics, pipe cleaners and a nappy pin. Although based on a pet rabbit, this piece is embellished with imagination.

SPOTLIGHT: Cathy Cullis

Cathy Cullis creates machine-stitched drawings, with faces and people drawn from imagination, which are evocative of medieval paintings and icons. She works mainly in paint and so uses the sewing machine in quite a painterly, fluid way. Her stitched work reflects that of her mark-making in paint.

Cathy has developed her own stitching style over the past few years. She is self-taught and does not consider herself to be a textile artist, just using the machine as a drawing tool. She works intuitively, never planning in detail. Her embroidery is inspired by historical paintings and the folk art of the past. Each small embroidery piece is an individual artwork containing many tiny, dancing stitches. Cathy works with a wide range of media, yet her focus is always on memory and storytelling.

< ^ *Dreamer Brooches* by Cathy Cullis. Cathy's work comes from her imagination but she is inspired by historical references.

Drawing from photographs

We will consider photography in detail in a later chapter (see page 74), but in terms of drawing, this is the method I use most in my own work. Photographs are ideal for capturing a person in movement, or people out and about. They allow you to still the movement and to explore the people you see when you come to use them as the basis for stitch drawing.

When making stitched drawings of people from photographs, there are five main steps:

1   Take photographs on a digital camera.
2   View the image on screen and make a selection.
3   Print out the photograph.
4   Trace the photograph (or draw the image from the photograph) on to cloth.
5   Stitch.

Drawbacks

A drawing made from a photograph will have a certain kind of style, which I think makes it obvious that it has come from a photograph (particularly so if you trace directly from the photograph). There is a kind of removal of the artist's hand, an almost mechanical effect to the drawing. When stitching is incorporated, the mechanical effect of the sewing machine emphasizes this. This combination creates a particular look, which stitched drawings often have.

Taking photographs of people

There are all sorts of possibilities. You could start by getting a friend to pose for you, but really the advantage of a camera is its ability to still movement, so ask your friend to do something.

If your digital camera has a continuous shooting mode, turn it on. Once you press the shutter, it will take pictures one after the other until you take your finger off the shutter. (If you set the file size of the image as small, the camera will be able to take continuous photographs more quickly.) The advantage of continuous shooting is that it will generate a lot of photographs to choose from later.

^ Detail from *The New Photographers* by Rosie James. This work was drawn from photographs of people taking photographs of *Mona Lisa* at the Louvre in Paris. I prefer to use photographs as a reference rather than tracing them.

In my own work, I look for crowds of people to photograph. I then stand somewhere discreet and take a lot of photographs using continuous shooting mode.

Selecting a subject

When you get back home, load the photographs on to your computer and look through them. Pick out the figures that interest you and which capture some feeling of the crowd and the rush, perhaps. Print out the photograph that appeals most.

The relevant parts of the image now need to be transferred to cloth, in order to stitch. You can use a number of methods to do this (see pages 46–47).

Transformation

During the steps between taking a photograph and creating a stitched artwork, an image goes through a transformative process.

- The photograph itself captures a precise moment; it is a representation of a person at a fleeting point in time.
- The image on the computer screen consists of a grid of pixels. The person in the photograph has become a flicker on a screen.
- The printout of the image reduces the person to dots of ink on paper. The image may have been cropped, re-sized and manipulated before printing.
- The traced drawing on the printout selects certain lines to best express the figure in the photograph. The ink dots have been reduced again to just a few lines.
- Finally, the stitched lines on the cloth try to follow the pencilled guidelines chosen from the image but may wobble about and go off course here and there, changing the final image one more time.

The process develops from an actual person to a photograph on a camera, to an image on a computer screen, to a print of the photograph, to the tracing of the photograph, to the transfer on to cloth, to the final stitching. So by the time a stitched drawing emerges on the chosen surfaces, the original person would probably not recognize himself!

^ Detail from *The New Photographers* by Rosie James. Would these people recognise themselves in stitch?

The end result

The first stitched drawing I made using photographs was from pictures I took at a friend's outdoor party by the sea, in front of her beach hut. I took lots of pictures and then stitched some of them and put them together in one piece. Some friends recognized themselves and others didn't; some liked their stitched doppelganger and others didn't. So be careful when stitching friends or people you know, and warn them that the end result can be quite different to what they might expect.

This piece consists of lots of individual pieces put together in one arrangement, including people sitting, standing, eating, talking and sitting on blankets or chairs, as well as a dog and a plate of food. The whole gives us an impression of the different activities going on.

For more detailed information about how to draw from photographs and how to transfer these drawings, see Photography for Stitch, page 74.

< ˅ *The Hut, Tankerton Slopes* (left) and close-up detail (below) by Rosie James. This stitched memento of a party at a beach hut was based on a compilation of photographs from the event.

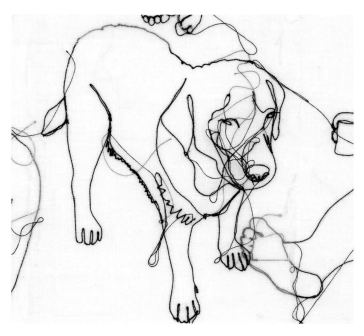

Drawing day

Put aside a whole day to concentrate on doing not much else but drawing. The exercises below should make it fun: start with number 1 and work your way through as many as possible, or just dip in and try a few. You will end up with a whole pile of drawings to use in future projects and it will help to get your drawing mind in gear. I have included some examples by the illustrator Mags James to give you the general idea. She has mostly used a fine-line pen or a pencil.

Remember to look hard at what is in front of you, and to look more at the object than at the paper. Some drawings you will be happy with, others not so much, but make sure you keep them all. As the day goes on, your drawings will become more confident in line and composition.

1   When you wake up, sit up in bed and draw the end of the bed and its surroundings.
2   Make a cup of tea and draw the mug or cup in between sips.
3   Decide what to wear. Lay these clothes out flat (or put them on a hanger and hang them on the wall) and draw them. Include underwear, socks and shoes.
4   Have a shower. When you've finished, draw the towels on the towel rail or bathroom floor.
5   Make breakfast and draw it.
6   Go to the nearest shop and buy something such as milk or a newspaper. Bring it home and draw it; draw the receipt as well.
7   Make lunch and draw it.
8   Put the radio on and draw it, along with the objects that surround it.
9   Sit facing a window and draw whatever you see within the frame of the window. It may be more interesting to draw the window's surroundings than what you can see through it.
10 Open a door into a room and sit outside that room looking through the door. Draw the door and what you can see beyond it.
11 Invite a friend round for a cup of tea and draw her as she drinks it.
12 Put the TV on and draw what's on the screen. Freeze-frame it if you can, or draw it as it changes.
13 Cook your evening meal, but before you do, get out all the ingredients and all the tools required to cook it and draw them.
14 Draw other people eating the meal.
15 Draw people relaxing and watching the TV.
16 Time for bed. Before you get into bed, crumple the bedclothes and draw them. Good night!

< ˅ Drawings completed by Mags James and Rosie James in a drawing day (see opposite).

Recording special events

We make drawings for all kinds of reasons, whether with a pencil or a sewing machine. Sometimes it's in order to look really closely at something or to give ourselves time to think in depth about an idea; at other times it's an opportunity to allow our imagination to wander. Occasionally, however, we may want to use drawings as a means of recording something in our life that we want to remember, just as we use photographs.

Consider then, using stitch drawing as a way of recording a significant event such as a holiday, a birth, a wedding or even a death. Textiles and stitching have been used to record these things throughout history. As mentioned earlier, the Bayeux Tapestry tells the story of a historic battle. At one time, young women created samplers of stitch to practise stitching and also as a way of recording their age, the date that the sampler was worked, who their family was, or occasionally their private thoughts. The earliest surviving samplers date from the fifteenth and sixteenth centuries.

Weddings

A stitched drawing can bring together different elements of an event in one piece, such as this work created to celebrate a wedding.

It was created using photographs taken by people at the wedding. It is composed of groups of people as they would have posed for photographs for each other. Photographs of the venue, including the ice-cream van and the beautiful garden, were screen-printed on to a linen background, in colours that reflected the venue and surroundings. The happy couple feature in stitch as the main focus, with guests stitched around them.

I appliquéd fabrics to the background using Bondaweb (see page 94). The fabrics were chosen for their likeness to the actual fabrics worn on the day, either in colour or pattern or both. I worked machine-stitched drawings on transparent cloth (such as cotton organdie) and then hand-stitched this on top of the appliquéd fabric sections.

> *Ripley Wedding* by Rosie James. Here, machine stitch is combined with screen printing and appliqué.

Stitching basics

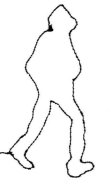

Now it's time to start stitching. In this chapter, we will get to grips with your sewing machine. Be prepared to experiment a little, change the settings and see what happens. Every sewing machine is different – let's see what yours does.

Sewing machine

Now that you have loads of drawings and have mastered the art of looking and using a pencil to draw with, let's move on to stitching. This is where you need to dig out that sewing machine and really get to know it.

Choosing a sewing machine

There are many different types of sewing machines out there and you should be able to do free-machine stitching on most of them, apart from very old antique models. Free-machine stitching is when you operate a machine with the feed dogs lowered (feed dogs are the mechanism that feeds the fabric past the needle), which allows you to manoeuvre the fabric (held in a hoop) freely under the needle.

My favourites are the older machines, which won't move as you sew and have a good engine on them. You don't need any fancy stitches – just straight stitch and zigzag will do. If you do not have a machine already, it is best to borrow someone else's and have a go. This will allow you to see whether this is something you want to do more of before committing to buying one, and it will also mean that you get a better idea of what you need a machine to do.

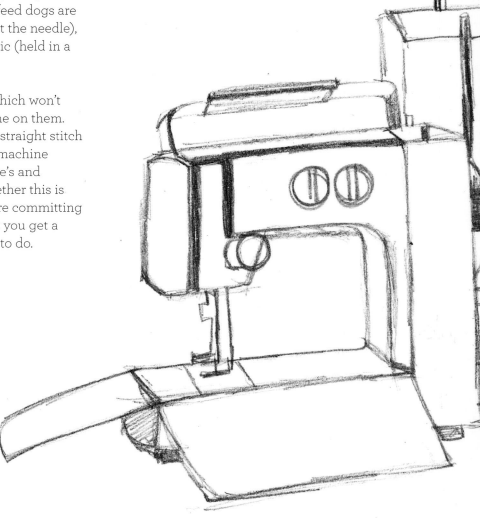

> Choose a sewing machine that you can operate with the feed dogs lowered.

If you are going to buy a new machine, go for a reliable make at a reasonable price (£100–£200), such as a Janome or a Singer. Check that you can do free-machine stitching and anything else that you fancy trying. Some new machines can be a bit restrictive in what they will allow you to do in terms of bobbin access and even stitch length.

A second-hand machine can sometimes be better than a new one, in that older machines are more solid and allow you to access the bobbin and to make alterations to the set up. There are plenty of second-hand machines for sale online. Look for old Berninas made in the 1960s or 1970s: these are very solid and basic and don't do any fancy stitches, but they do allow you to drop the feed dogs (more below), which is perfect for machine embroidery. However, these machines are very sought after and usually go for £150 upwards, depending on the condition.

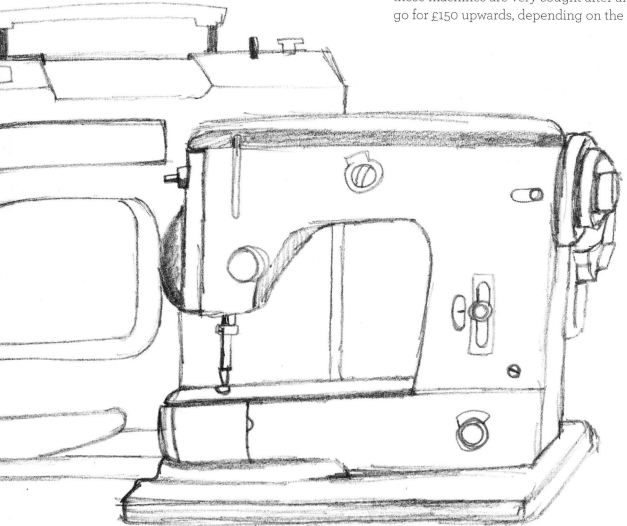

Setting up a sewing machine

Consult the manual of the sewing machine for basic setting up and threading instructions. The reel of thread goes on a spool pin on top of the machine (I refer to this as the top thread); thread is also wound on to a bobbin that is placed in the bobbin case that lurks underneath the needle (the bottom thread).

There are four things you need to remember to set up on the machine which relate specifically to free-machine embroidery.

1 Lower the feed dogs

The feed dogs are the teeth-like parts under the needle that move fabric along as you sew. We want to give the fabric a smooth ride, so we need to lower them out of the way. Some machines have a lever or button that does this.

If the machine does not have a lever, you can cover the feed dogs with a darning plate. A darning plate is a flat, square piece of plastic that clips over the feed dog area, leaving a hole for the needle.

If you do not have a darning plate, you can stick a piece of paper over the feed dogs, leaving a small hole for the needle.

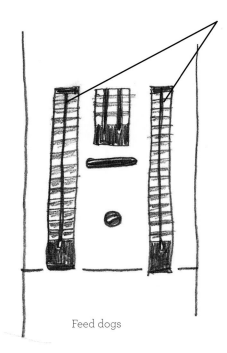

The feed dogs sit under the stitch plate. Lower them for free-machine embroidery.

Feed dogs

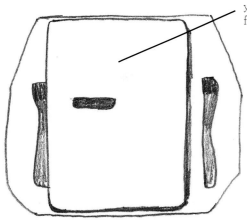

Use a darning plate if you cannot lower the feed dogs.

Darning plate

2 Set the stitch length to zero

The reason for this is that you are going to be altering the stitch length as you move the fabric about underneath the needle. We don't want to restrict the machine in any way. You will find that if you move the fabric quickly under the needle, you will get long stitches; move it more slowly and the stitches will be shorter.

All machines have some sort of stitch length setting: if you cannot set it on zero, set it as low as you can.

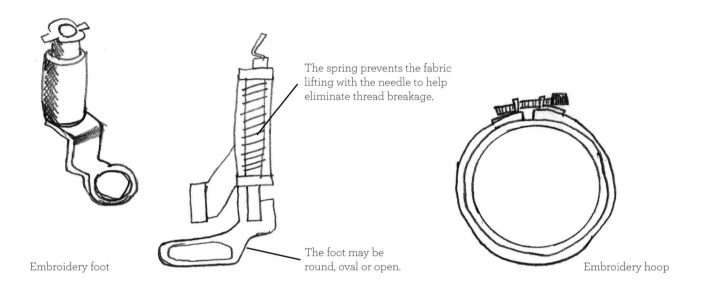

The spring prevents the fabric lifting with the needle to help eliminate thread breakage.

The foot may be round, oval or open.

Embroidery foot

Embroidery hoop

3 Attach an embroidery foot

There are a huge variety of feet available for sewing machines, which do all kinds of things. For our purposes, you need an embroidery foot (or a darning foot or a quilting foot). You may find that one came with your machine, but if not, look in a haberdashery shop or online for the right attachment.

You can, of course, do free-machine stitching without a foot, just leaving the needle free. However, you will find that this means that you cannot tell whether the presser foot is up or down, and it is very important that the presser foot is down when you start to sew.

The purpose of a foot is to stop the fabric from bouncing up and down the needle as you sew, but it also acts as a safety element, as it stops you from putting your fingers under the needle.

4 Use a hoop

An embroidery hoop consists of two wooden rings, one fitting tightly inside the other. It holds the cloth taut, creating a drum-like effect. Place the smaller hoop on a flat surface and lay the fabric over it. Put the other hoop on top and press them together. Use the screw to tighten it up, and then go round the edge pulling the cloth taut as you go. Keep going until you get it as tight as a tambourine.

It is important to use a hoop as it will enable you to move the cloth freely under the needle, which will result in a better drawing. It also prevents puckering. (If you are using quite thick fabric, you may not need a hoop; if you are using something like paper, a hoop is not necessary at all.) If you are using very fine, slithery fabric, you can wrap the inner ring of the hoop with a strip of cloth to give it extra grip.

Getting started

Let's begin stitch drawing. To start with, use a fairly sturdy fabric such as calico in the hoop.

1 Put the hoop under the foot so that the fabric is flat on the surface of the machine and the hoop is like a well. Make sure it is not the other way round, or you will have a gap between the fabric and surface of the sewing machine.

2 Position the needle over a point where you want to start. For this first attempt, start in the middle. Lower the presser foot (this engages the tension).

3 I always start by lowering the needle into the cloth by hand. Grip the hoop on both sides, then put your foot on the foot pedal and as the engine starts and the needle begins to rise and fall, move the hoop. Push the hoop around in any direction as the needle is in motion and the stitched line will go where you go. If you stop moving the hoop, take your foot off the pedal – otherwise the machine will carry on stitching in the same place and you'll get a huge, knotty mess.

4 Create a doodle of circles and scribble to allow you to get the feel of the sewing machine. Try moving fast and slowly and in different directions.

5 When you have finished, take your foot off the pedal and stop moving the hoop. Pull the hoop out from under the foot and snip off the threads, leaving a thread tail of about 5cm (2in).

6 Separate the rings of the hoop and remove the fabric. Now put a new piece of calico in the hoop and try doing another doodle, but this time try actually writing something, such as your name. This allows you to do something specific but without having to stop and start.

7 When you have done that and feel a bit more confident with the machine, try doing a simple drawing. Draw directly on the calico with a pencil: something simple like a flower. Position the hoop so that the drawing is in the middle. Take the needle down somewhere on the pencil line and then start sewing, following the line carefully.

8 When you come to the end of the line and need to restart elsewhere, simply lift the presser foot and pull the top thread to one side while moving the hoop to reposition the needle at a new starting point. Lower the presser foot and start again. Do this every time you need to move. You can snip off the thread tails when you have finished or leave them loose for that scribbly, loose drawing effect shown in the examples on page 55 and 57.

9 Now you have got the hang of using the sewing machine to draw a line, you can move on to more complicated drawings. Look through the drawings from your drawing day (see page 24) or at some of your figure drawings (see page 14) and start there.

> To get started, use a sturdy fabric such as calico, and position the hoop to keep the fabric steady while working.

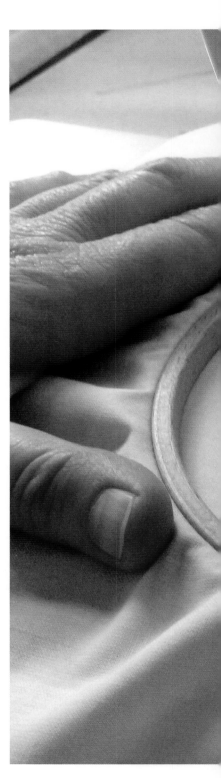

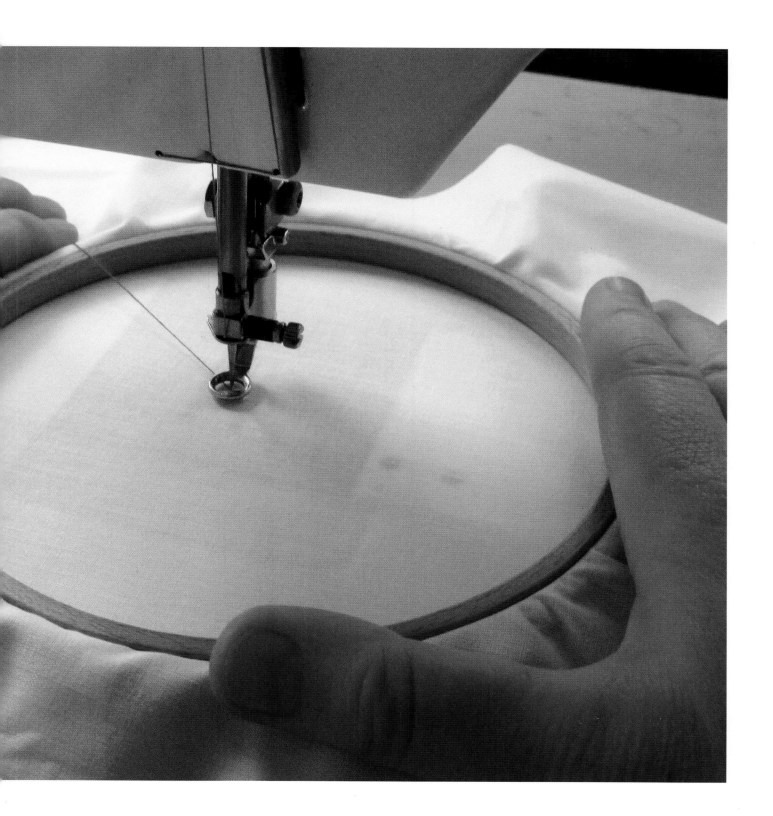

Experimenting with your machine

Now that you have managed to create a simple line drawing, you can begin to experiment a bit with your sewing machine and see what other kinds of lines and marks it will make. You can use different threads to stitch with and try different surfaces to stitch on, but also play around with the actual machine itself.

All machines are different: some machines will do certain things and others will not, so be careful – you do not want to damage the machine permanently. Just make sure that it is possible to change things back to the way that they were before.

Tension

One of the most exciting elements you can experiment with is the tension.

A sewing machine has two tensions in play: the tension of the top reel of thread and the tension of the bottom bobbin. Use the dial on the front of the machine to loosen or tighten the top thread (you may need to check the manual that came with the machine to locate the tension dial). It is usually numbered from 1 to 10; 5 represents normal tension and 10 is the tightest tension. Or you may simply have a dial with a '+' or '–' to indicate tighter or looser tension.

If you look at the manual, you will probably find a diagram similar to the one shown right. This shows you the effects of altering the tension. If you tighten the tension of the top thread, you will find the bottom thread gets pulled to the top; if you loosen the top thread tension, you will find that the top thread gets pulled to the underside of the cloth and can get loopy.

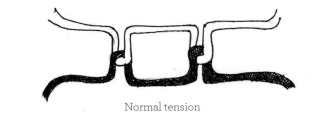

Normal tension

Tightened top thread

Loosened top thread

Experiment with your machine and see what happens. Put some cloth in the hoop and stitch a line, then turn the tension dial to increase the tension and stitch another line. Now compare the two. Slacken the tension and stitch again; compare the three different lines. Look at both sides of the cloth: did you get a loopy mess? Was it difficult to handle? Did the cloth get stuck? If any of these things happen, try altering the tension in smaller increments to effect more subtle changes that might be easier to control.

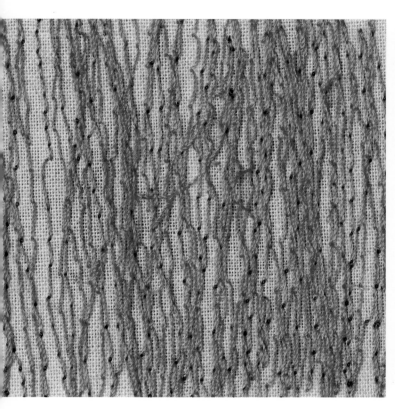

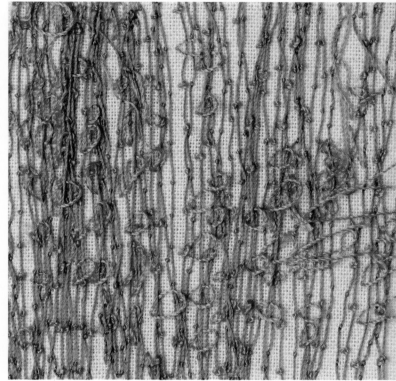

^ In the sample above, the top tension was set as low as it can go. The top thread was orange and the bottom thread was blue – the blue thread has been pulled up a little, and is just visible as tiny dots. Different machines will have slightly different effects and the lowering of the top tension to its lowest level may cause the lower thread to be completely invisible from the top.

^ If we look at the back of the sample shown left, we see the loopy effect created by the looseness of the orange top thread. This loopy effect is good if you want to fill in an area with a bit of colour and texture in a kind of scribbly, painterly way.

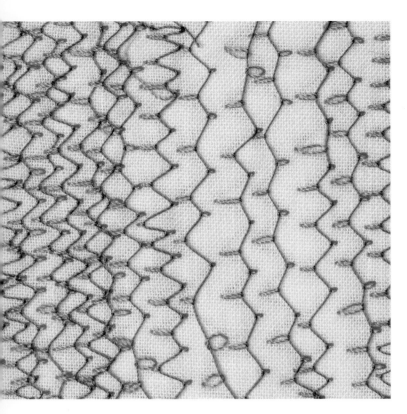 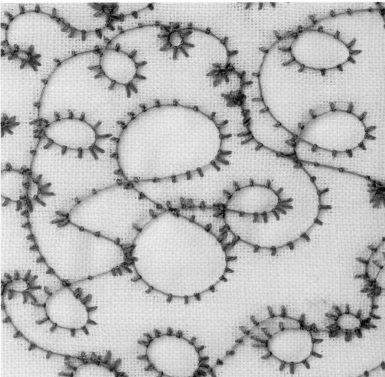

While you are experimenting with the tension dial, don't just stitch in a straight line but take the opportunity to see what happens when you change the direction of the line or create curves. Try out a different stitch or two on your machine as well, working with simple stitches such as zigzag.

In the sample above right, the top thread is orange and the bottom thread is blue. Notice how the tight tension of the orange thread pulls up the bottom blue thread, giving the appearance of short blue stitches at right angles to the orange line. This effect is more pronounced on the curves.

In the sample above left, it is the blue thread that is now on top and the orange thread is in the bobbin. The high top tension has the same effect on this open zigzag stitch as when stitching curves and the lower thread is brought up to form contrasting horizontal stitches.

∧ In the sample above right, the curves put even greater tension on the upper orange thread, pulling the blue bobbin thread into longer stitches on the surface. This effect would also look good if both the top and bobbin threads were the same colour.

In the sample above left, the open zigzag stitch is worked with blue thread on top and orange thread in the bobbin. You can clearly see the loops created as the bobbin thread is pulled up due to the tight tension on the upper thread.

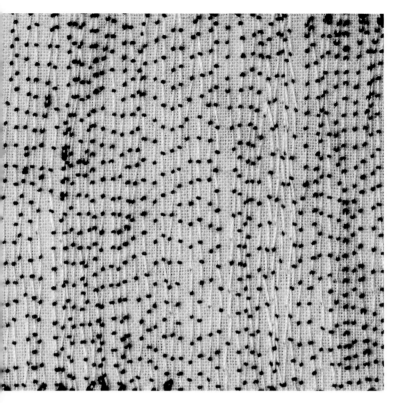

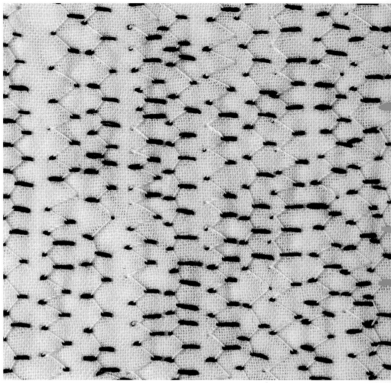

The colour of the threads also has a visual effect. Black and white threads on white cotton can give a dotty line or a peppered effect. The sample above left is straight stitch with a tight top tension, and the one above right is the same in zigzag. The white threads blend in with the background and just leave the black marks visible. The white thread is on the top and the black in the bobbin.

The tension of the lower thread is more difficult to alter and on some machines this cannot be altered at all. It is not normally necessary to alter the tension on the lower thread as it can all be controlled from the top. However, you may want to experiment with it a bit to see what different effects you can get. Find out how to do this overleaf.

> When the top thread matches the fabric and the top tension is tight, a contrasting bottom thread is brought to the top to create a dotted line for this monogram.

^ In the sample above left the white top thread is set to a high tension. The black bobbin thread is brought up to the top and the result looks as if white thread has been couched with black.

The sample above right is the same but with a zig zag stitch. The white thread almost vanishes and the result is an attractive speckling.

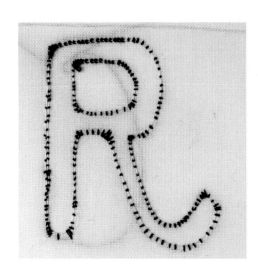

Bobbin tension

The lower thread is wound on a bobbin, which is placed in a bobbin case. The bobbin case is not removable on most of the machines manufactured today; however older machines will allow you to do so.

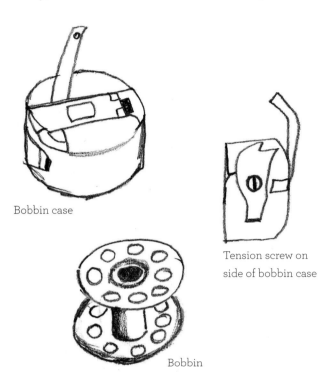

Bobbin case

Tension screw on side of bobbin case

Bobbin

If you can remove the bobbin case, you will see a small screw on one side; this is the tension screw. The tension of the lower thread can be loosened by using a small screwdriver to turn the screw one-quarter of a turn to the left (hold the bobbin case exactly as it is in the above drawing). Turn a quarter-turn to the right in order to increase the tension. You must be very careful not to unscrew the screw completely, as it is very tiny and will drop to the floor and then you will never see it again (believe me!).

In order to return to normal tension, you need to return the screw to its original position. You may want to keep a separate bobbin case especially for playing about with, so that when you return to normal sewing you can put the original case back in.

Thick threads

When drawing with a sewing machine, we are stitching a line. The thickness of this line depends on the thickness of the thread, and the thickness of the thread depends on the size of the eye of the needle. If you buy needles which are designed for metallic threads, the eye is quite large and will allow you to use a slightly thicker thread than normal.

However, if you want to use something even thicker, try putting it on the bobbin and working from the back. Load up the bobbin with thread (start with some fine wool, perhaps) and alter the tension so that the thread can flow through the bobbin smoothly. Be careful not to turn the tension screw too much; you don't want it to fall out. Experiment with different thicknesses of thread and see what the machine will tolerate – and what it won't.

Put the cloth in the hoop as usual and follow the lines of your drawing. The thick thread is underneath so the actual work will be upside down. Take it slowly at first; you may need to alter the top tension as well. On completion, turn the work over to see the final result. You should find that the thick thread has created a raised line on the surface of the cloth. You will also find that thick threads work best on simple drawings, as you cannot cross over lines easily or have too many lines near each other.

< This close-up detail of the sample above clearly shows the white top thread and the thicker blue thread of the bobbin. Just trim excess threads with sharp scissors; you cannot pull them through to the other side as they are too thick. Experiment with the top tension and the speed at which you sew. A faster speed and small movements will move the white top stitches closer together.

^ In this sample, the top thread was white cotton and the bobbin thread was a blue perle thread normally used for hand embroidery. The sample was worked from the other side, so the blue thread was not visible. The white top thread acts as a couching thread, holding the thicker thread down. Use threads of the same colour if you do not want the top thread to be visible.

Inspiration from art history

When thinking about drawing with a sewing machine instead of a pen or pencil, it's interesting to look at work by the masters of drawing – from the Renaissance to contemporary art. Study the kinds of marks they make and consider how this could be done with a sewing machine or with stitch. Artists you could look at include Leonardo da Vinci, Michelangelo and Dürer.

Leonardo da Vinci uses lots of lines and hatching – all of which could be re-created in stitch. Michelangelo's studies for the Sistine Chapel were drawn with red chalk, which creates a slight fuzziness; you can also get this effect with some threads, in particular cheap polyester cotton threads. Re-create the effect by stitching in rusty red on a creamy background cloth.

^ < This is the stitched drawing that I made (above) and a close-up detail (left). The original drawing is probably quite small; this stitched version is about 90 x 60cm (35½ x 23½in).

Albrecht Dürer's hands

I decided to use one of Albrecht Dürer's hand studies, *Study of the Hands*, as the basis for a stitch drawing, selecting one particular hand because it looks as if it is holding a piece of thread. In order to re-create it, I scanned it and enlarged it, then transferred the marks on to cloth ready for stitching.

Dürer used his pen to create different thicknesses of line. To do this on a sewing machine, you can go over a line a few times until you get the thickness you want. It is much cruder than the subtlety of the pen, but an interesting mark. I left the threads loose to create a scribbly effect, but also to emphasize that fact this is a drawing stitched with a sewing machine and not drawn with a pen and ink.

From drawings to stitch drawings

Now you have some interesting drawings, and you have got to grips with your sewing machine, it's time to stitch those drawings. In this chapter we will look at a variety of ways to transfer those drawings to cloth.

Transferring a drawing

In order to start stitching, you need to transfer a drawing from your sketchbook on to the surface on which you are going to stitch. There are various ways of doing this, depending on the nature of the substance to be stitched on: you can use transparent cloth, transfer pencils, transfer paper, water-soluble fabric or paper, and tissue paper.

Transparent cloth

This is perhaps the most direct method and the one I use the most, simply because stitching on transparent fabric allows you to layer up images and move things around when thinking about composition.

Use a fabric such as silk organza or cotton organdy, both of which are completely transparent and easy to draw on. Polyester voile is cheaper, but is more slithery to draw on. You could also try using white polyester cotton: the cheap ones are usually quite see-through.

First, scale up the drawing to the size you require. You can either use a photocopier to do this or scan it into the computer and enlarge it. Cut out a piece of fabric, making it larger than the drawing to allow room for the hoop. Place the drawing on a flat, hard surface and use masking tape to hold it in place. Put the transparent fabric over the top, placing the image in the middle. Now use a sharp pencil to trace over the lines of your drawing to transfer them on to the cloth. Put the cloth in the hoop and stitch (see page 48 for a step-by-step example). Bear in mind that although the pencilled lines will not wash out, the stitched lines should cover them completely.

Transfer pencils and pens

If you want to transfer a drawing on to fabric that is not transparent, you could try transfer pencils or pens, which allow you to draw the image on a transparent paper (tracing paper or tissue paper) and then transfer it by ironing on to the fabric. The heat from the iron transfers the line of the pen to the cloth. These pens and pencils are available from haberdashery stores and online and come in a variety of colours. The marks made by the pens do not wash out.

One thing to bear in mind is that the image will become reversed, so to counteract this, first reverse the image using a photocopier or printer.

Tissue paper is easier to iron than tracing paper. You will also find that the image transfers better on some fabrics than others. You need a steady hand with the iron and a hot setting, so fine, synthetic fabrics may not be suitable for this method.

Transfer paper

Transfer paper is a coated paper available in a range of colours. To use it, place your fabric on a hard surface and then put the paper on top, coloured-side down. Draw an image on the paper using a pointed implement such as a pencil (you have to press down hard enough for the coating of the paper to transfer to the cloth). This method works best on quite smooth fabrics.

Water-soluble fabric or paper

All the methods described opposite leave you with a line on the cloth that does not wash off; if this is a problem, you may want to try using water-soluble fabric. This is available in large sheets or by the metre. Trace the drawing on to it as you would any transparent fabric, being careful not to tear it. When you are ready to stitch, position it over the fabric, put the two layers in the hoop and stretch them tight. Stitch over the lines and when completely finished, wash the fabric and the water-soluble layer will simple disappear.

This method is best for any fabrics with a bit of texture or whenever you don't want visible pen lines. However, you need cloth that is washable.

Tissue paper

To use tissue paper for image transfer, first trace the image on to the tissue paper using an ordinary pencil. Place the tissue paper over the fabric and put the two layers in the hoop, being careful not to rip the tissue paper in the process.

Now stitch along the lines through both the tissue paper and the fabric. When you have completed the stitching, remove the hoop and then gently rip the tissue paper away. Be careful not to pull too hard, or you will remove some of the stitching. This method works well on a variety of surfaces (see Surfaces, page 56).

< You don't have to remove all the tissue paper, of course. Here I left some in to create a slightly different colour inside the stitched figure.

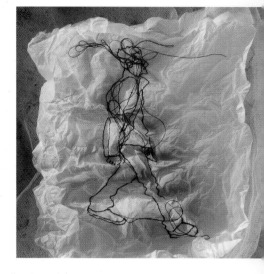

> This figure was stitched on to net using the tissue-paper method. The photograph shows it before the tissue paper was removed, but you could leave it there and make the most of its scrunching quality.

˅ The final drawing: the tissue paper has been removed with a few bits left in to add interest.

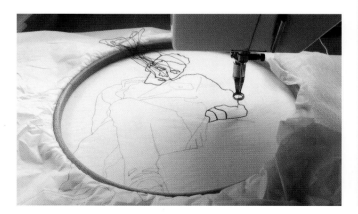

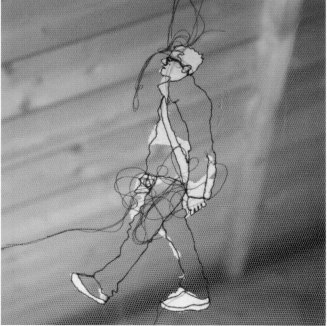

Your first stitch drawing

You should have a huge pile of lovely drawings on paper from your drawing day (see page 24), and now we are going to stitch one of them. For your first stitched drawing, it makes it easier if you choose a fairly simple drawing – one that does not have too many scribbly lines or shading.

I have chosen the work I did for the exercise of drawing the view through a window, in which I chose to draw the window and the items around it rather than what I could see through it. The drawing was done in pencil in an A4 sketchbook.

1 To make the drawing even easier to stitch, you may want to make it bigger. Small drawings are usually harder to stitch as the threads are more likely to get tangled up and it is more difficult to see what you are doing. I decided to increase the size of my drawing to A3 (scan and re-size on a computer or use a photocopier to do this).

2 The next step is to transfer the drawing to cloth. There are various methods for doing this (see page 46), but for this piece I traced my photocopied and enlarged drawing on to silk organza using a sharp HB pencil.

3 Cut out a piece of fabric bigger than the drawing, allowing about 8cm (3¼in) around the drawing for the hoop. Attach the drawing to a smooth surface and tape the fabric over the top, with the drawing in the middle. Trace it, making sure that the fabric doesn't move.

> The finished piece is stitched on silk organza, then laid over white canvas, which has screenprinted sections where the window is.

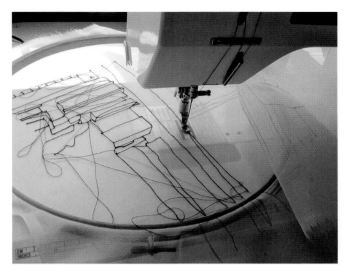

4 Now you are ready to stitch. Position the hoop in one corner and once you have stitched all the lines in the hoop, reposition it over another section and stitch all those lines. Keep moving the hoop until you have completed the whole thing.

5 Snip off all the loose threads or leave them if you want a scribbly effect.

So there you have it: a drawing from your sketchbook has now become a stitched drawing on cloth. You may want to try stitching the same drawing using a variety of different fabrics and transfer methods, to see the different effects they have on the drawing.

A stitched figure drawing

Now try a different kind of drawing, using tissue paper to transfer the image. Choose one of your figure drawings (see page 14). I am going to transfer an A5 drawing from my sketchbook.

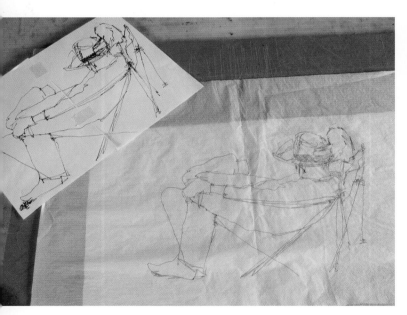

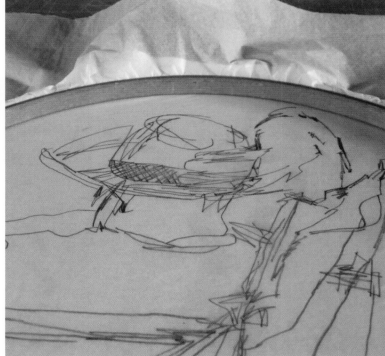

1 Enlarge the drawing if you wish (I scanned the image and enlarged it to A3), then print it out. Trace the printed image or photocopy on to a sheet of tissue paper.

2 Layer the tissue paper over the cloth you are going to stitch on and insert the double thickness into a hoop. Make sure you position the drawing with enough space around the edge the get the hoop on.

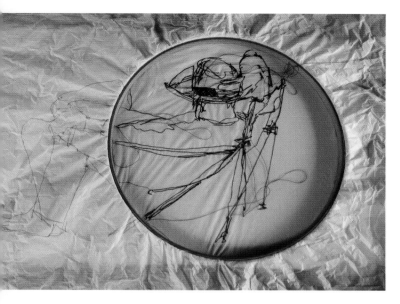

3 Stitch along the lines (in this kind of loose sketch, it doesn't matter so much if you veer off the lines). You may need to stitch it in parts, moving the hoop once you have filled in one section.

4 Once finished, remove the tissue paper or leave bits of it in place if you like the effect.

5 The finished stitched piece is shown below. Once you have completed your stitched figure drawing you can, if you wish, stretch your work over a frame in order to hang it on the wall, or mount it on a piece of mounting board and frame it under glass (see Presenting Your Work, page 110, for ideas on displaying your work).

Draw your clothes

One fun way to get stitch-drawing is to choose some clothes that have interesting elements such as collars, large buttons, flounces or frills. To achieve a good viewpoint, put the item(s) on a coat hanger and then hang this on the wall. Sit in front of the garment with your sketchbook to draw it. Alternatively, you could just lay the garment out flat on the floor and look down on it.

1 Keep the drawing simple, drawing mainly outlines and just a few details and folds or creases. In this drawing I included the hanger, otherwise it looked as if the skirt was floating in space.

2 Transfer the image and stitch the lines of the drawing as previously described. My drawing of a skirt was a good one to stitch, as it was not too complicated yet got its subject across well.

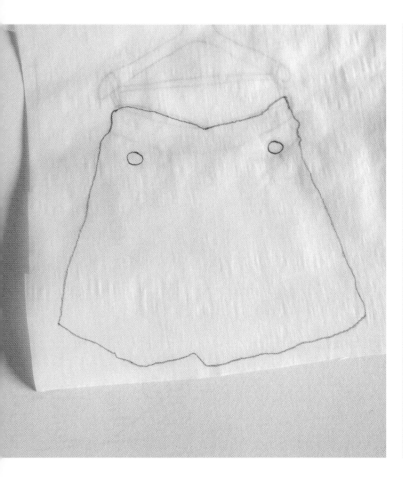

3 How about adding some colour to the garment? You will need some coloured fabric and some Bondaweb (see page 94). First, cut out a square of Bondaweb bigger than the drawing. Place it over the drawing, paper-side up, and trace around the area you wish to fill with colour.

4 Place on the wrong side of your chosen fabric, webbing-side down. Separate the paper backing from the sheet of glue, flip over and replace over the glue before fusing. If you do not do this, the fabric will be a mirror image of the drawing.

5 Iron the square of Bondaweb (you are ironing the backing paper) on to the wrong side of the fabric following the manufacturer's instructions. Cut out the shape using sharp scissors.

6 Attach the cut-out shape to the cloth being used for the background: peel away the backing and then iron it on.

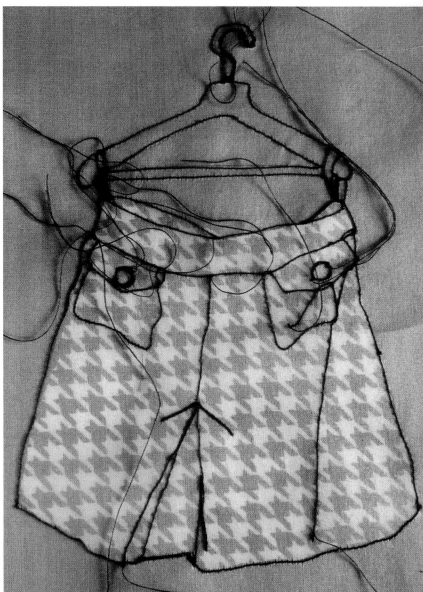

7 Once the shape has been attached, you could stitch your drawing directly on to the top of it. Alternatively, stitch on to transparent fabric and then lay this on top of the background fabric. The transparent cloth will completely cover the coloured shape and so will make it slightly paler. Consider different types and colours of background fabric too, before sticking the shape down – once stuck it cannot be removed.

8 Now empty out the rest of your wardrobe and create a whole collection of stitched drawings of all your clothes!

Surfaces

Drawings do not just have to be made with pencil on paper; sewing does not just have to be thread on cloth. It is possible to stitch on all kinds of different surfaces and substances; you just need to experiment to see what it is possible to feed through your sewing machine. These are just a few examples to get you started.

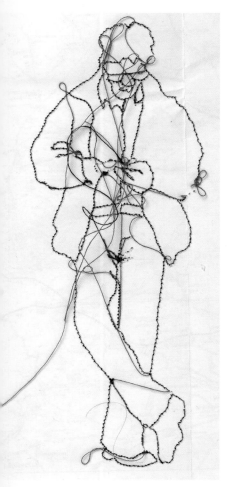

< I used red thread in the bobbin and black for the top thread. You can see this if we look at the back of the drawing.

ᵛ > On the front of the drawing, the red bobbin thread appears as a series of dots.

Paper

There are many different types of paper and the possibilities for exploration are endless. Look for printed papers or print your own.

When transferring an image you could simply draw on the paper, or print on it and then stitch the lines. The best method, though, is to use the tissue-paper method of transferring the image (see page 47). The tissue paper gives another layer of protection and can add to the final artwork.

Things to bear in mind when stitching on paper
- Don't use a hoop. You don't need one, and a hoop would rip the paper.
- Paper can blunt needles, so after sewing on paper, change the needle before you switch back to sewing on fabric.
- Be careful not to stitch too many lines next to each other, or the paper will rip and you'll get a big hole.
- Keep the drawing fairly simple and don't make it too small.

Maps are interesting to stitch on. Lay tissue paper over the map and stitch the lines without using a hoop.

Remove all or some of the tissue paper afterwards. In the close-up (left), you can see that the tissue paper has been removed from around the edges of the figure but some has been left inside the shape. This gives the figure an opaque quality and makes it more distinct from its background.

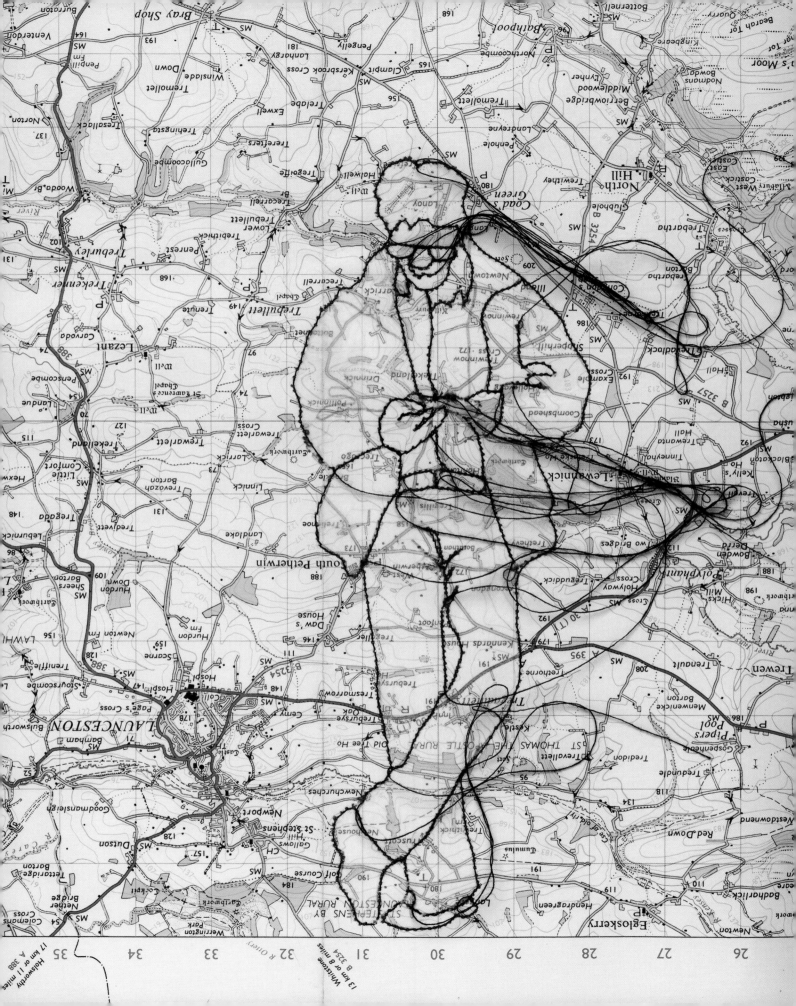

Day in the life of the gas price

Trades on the 'day ahead' market from 9am on 28 September 2012

e closing bell, the
. Final session of the
it's only the end of
New Gas Year: in the
ld, today's a seismic
month, end of the
season, and – deck
e gas year too. No
nervous. Day-ahead
cking. It was only
ent out my market
w it's down a full
ng into the final few

eenwich Mean Time
e yellow bar counting
on my right-hand
he call slips and walk
rop the E.ON one on
picks up when I dial,
d run-through of
ut on the curve.
Statoil, he's quick-
d they fire out their
wning 50-caliber
ly look at the others
own while I zigzag
G here, Gazprom
h for her, EDF for
f the oil price on
into the hot seat.
fuck? Jump out my
he Reuters terminal
chart looks properly
oil newsbar but the
o reason the price
ed like that from
straight reason, at

low opens at 16.00
open till 16.30, and
? Front-month con-
up nicely all day,
S employment data
ks, just a quiet one
eekend, then – bang
the front month
oor. Nosedives like
it in the fuselage,
d cat bounce, not
it plummets ever
to a penny that'll
the window shuts,
watching it till then,
in less than a minute, I've
e gas price.
faithful yellow bar, I
and scan the lefthand
slightly short, having
urs ago.
that would have
near term contracts
in the same month]
g into the close, but
those. 16.29.17; quick
nal Grid entry zone
the main pipeline
Norway – is still
a touch down from

as being pumped into
uefied natural gas
ic by comparison,
supply tightness
eady been factored
near curve
racts]

ds a text, timing
ll call back soon
prices are in. Can't
e dinner is, no time
now, it's almost
nce for luck, then

the curve. "Weekend 59.25-35, nothing
working days, October 59-59.3, Novem-
ber 61.95" ...
   I let my subconscious do the writing,
my mind's back on Day-ahead. When
he gets to summer '14 I say "thanks"
and let him go, don't really need any
more comment than the "hold on ...
it's collapsed" bit; day-ahead is what's
of most interest today, the rest pretty
bland given the market's situation. No one
wants to take proper positions ahead of
next week, when winter replaces summer and a new gas year begins.
   No numbers from Erro, but Sandro's
screenshot is in, I jot down the prices,
they're a pretty much perfect match
with Dan's. Day-ahead said, of course,
that one's all over the place. Sandro's
got 58.40 bid, 58.75 offered, last print
[trade] at 58.00, something's going
off there.
   Two minutes till the top, I'll check
Reuters again: wish I was a trader,
saw that one coming a mile off, it's
been and gone and Brent's off the
bounce again – soon as the free-trading
window shut, it reversed the losses,
insouciantly ticked up again like nothing had ever happened.
   Back at my desk I instant-message my
friend Kenny, a former price reporter.
"This market is so silent, isn't it."

days can throw up exceptional
storm zones etc ... Probably
believe it's easiest to manipulate on a Fri-
day ... which ...
   16.3 - 10: I call ICAP (a brokerage
which handles deals between energy
companies) on the line. "'Allo mate, wanna
run-through do ya" I murmur my
assent, he's already rattling off the
prices, not skipping a beat. "Day-
ahead 58, weekend 59.35, working ays
don't normally interrupt them, but
this time I'm intrigued. "Hold on, sorry,
that day-ahead, was that firm" He
sounds like he was expecting the query:
"Yeah that's where we had it close at it,
pretty likely"
   Next ... where unfortunately comes
into play why he'd say that to me, but I
keep schtum and let him go on. "It was
offered 58 at the time [16.30], then
0.05 seconds after was paid there," he
explains, I thank him, then he moves
onto the front month – "59s all right
dude, had a good 'un" – and he's gone,
I get onto Kenny on Yahoo and tell
him what we just heard. Kenny's reply:
"Classic"

   ot on. I bet they're taking the piss,
ds on they have something to do
ith that last second collapse. Trouble
, I can't ask them, Can't ask anyone
anything, to be honest – half the traders
only speak to us off the record, and the
other half aren't authorised by their
compliance departments to do anything
other than read out the numbers like
the talking clock, then I ang up.
   All my attention still on Day-ahead, I
go downstairs for a quick smoke before
the trades sheet arrives. Bet the price
recovered straight after 16.30, just like
oil did, and just like you'd expect if there
was a fix in the air. My instinct says
there's no way that was a fair quote at
58, the price never gives up half a penny
in a flash like that without something
being amiss.
   Back upstairs, ten to five, ICAP's
closing email sets the price – 59 –
that means the price did recover straight
away as predicted.
   17 ... closes come in, I open the
spreadsheet and none straight in on
Day-ahead Exhibit B: only six trades at
58, everything else screaming out that
the price should be more like 58.5. Heart
says ignore the suspicious ones, head
says call in the bosses. Let them take
the rap, that's what they're paid for. I

Short and mismatched
eth Freedman says price reporting
agencies use often relatively poorly
paid reporters to glean information
from typically highly paid and
partisan gas traders Photograph:
Linda Nylind for the Guardian

» **'Bang! Bang! Bang! Six times
people have tried to force the price
down'** Watch the whistleblower Seth
Freedman explain how gas prices
are set and describe the mysterious
sequence of trades on a key day of the
gas year that prompted him to raise
alarm bells about price manipulation
in the gas market

» **'Sometimes there's a feeling
that somebody is taking the piss
on the day ahead index'** Listen to
conversations recorded by Freedman
with gas traders in which they discuss
widespread suspicions that traders try
to manipulate index prices

» **'The worst things are those ... that
continually and deliberately say
they are seeing something that they
are not'** Read Freedman's internet
message conversation with a gas trader
who tells him "there are a few shops
that continually try and distort closes

How the market works

A £300bn business v

A domestic gas bill will
show the wholesale
price paid by the
supplier but give no
indication of how
that value has been
arrived at by British
Gas, EDF or whoever
serves the household or business. Big
energy firms traditionally buy much
of their future needs via longer term
contracts lasting three or more years
and costing billions of pounds. These
contracts were until recently linked to
the more transparent price of oil.
   Many European and east Asia gas
contracts are still tied to oil prices but
Britain has led the way in developing a
gas "market" where buyers and sellers
can come to trade. It is estimated by
the Financial Services Authority to be
worth about £300bn a year

quoted company's
its share price, dec
of gas contracts in
market is much ha
must subscribe to
of specialist agenc
culation based on
Prices set by these
important because
deals are based on
   Chris Cook, seni
at King's College L
director of the Inte
Exchange, says the
of the gas trading i
history. "It remind
days of the oil mar
dependent on cons
traders not talking
that is inevitably w
is a structural issue

< In this image we see how effective it can be to leave some of the tissue behind.

> A black plastic bag makes a dramatic background. Plastic can be a little slippery to stitch on but the tissue paper layer will help here, as well as showing you the lines to stitch along.

˅ The dramatic radiating lines of this cake wrapper help to focus attention on the stitched portrait.

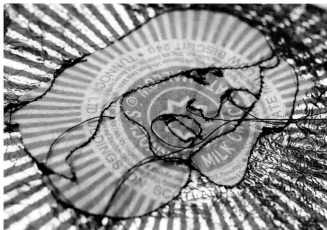

Newspaper is another good paper to use as a background 'fabric'. It is thin, but the tissue paper helps to stabilize it. You can also position your drawing in relation to the printed text in such a way as to make a point. Or you may want to stitch around particular images in the newspaper and add to them or comment on them.

We come across a huge variety of printed papers every day, all of which could be stitched on. Consider things such as receipts, packaging, wrapping paper, leaflets, bus tickets or rubbish.

Fabrics

There is, of course, a wide range of dressmaking and furnishing fabrics to stitch on. Here's a guide to what you can expect when you experiment on them. You will find that on a fine cloth, the stitched line sits on the surface of the fabric; with fabric of a medium thickness, the stitched line is not so raised; and with thick fabrics, such as felt or wool, the stitched line tends to sink into the surface.

Fine fabrics

I use silk organza a lot as it is transparent but has quite a dense weave and so is very strong. It grips a hoop well.

Silk habotai is also very fine, but not as transparent as silk organza. It has a lovely shine and is more slithery. With fine fabrics, you may need to bulk up the hoop by wrapping some tape or bias binding around it to help it to grip the fabric. Use a fine, sharp needle to stitch silk habotai.

Cotton organdy is very strong, transparent, and has a dense weave; it is a bit like silk organza but creases a lot. It has the feel and crunch of paper. It is a good choice as it will last longer than silk, but it is more expensive.

There are some very fine synthetics, such as voile. These tend to be more slithery than natural fibres but are cheaper. They can be a little more difficult to draw on with a pencil.

Mid-range fabrics

Fabrics of an average thickness are a good place to start, as they are the easiest to handle. These include natural-fibre products such as cotton calico, white cotton and linen; blends such as polyester cotton; and synthetics such as polyester. They all fit into the hoop well and are nice and smooth for stitching on.

Thick fabrics

This is where you may encounter some problems. Thick fabrics can be quite stiff, in which case you will not need a hoop at all. Materials such as leather and denim will need special needles for best results. Be careful when free-machining: don't try to stitch too fast or the needle will break.

Leather is actually quite easy to stitch on. Use a sheet of tissue paper underneath to prevent the leather sticking to the sewing machine and to assist in moving it around smoothly. You probably will not need a hoop.

Some thick fabrics, such as felt or blankets, are quite soft and floppy and you may still need a hoop. It's a good idea to use a thick thread in order for the stitched line to be seen, otherwise it will tend to sink into the surface. You could try placing a stabilizer,

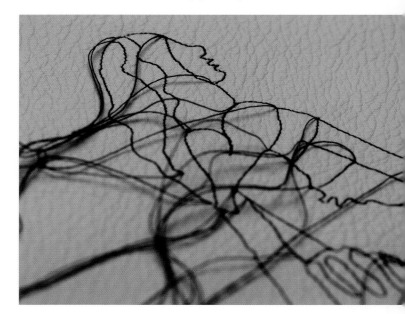

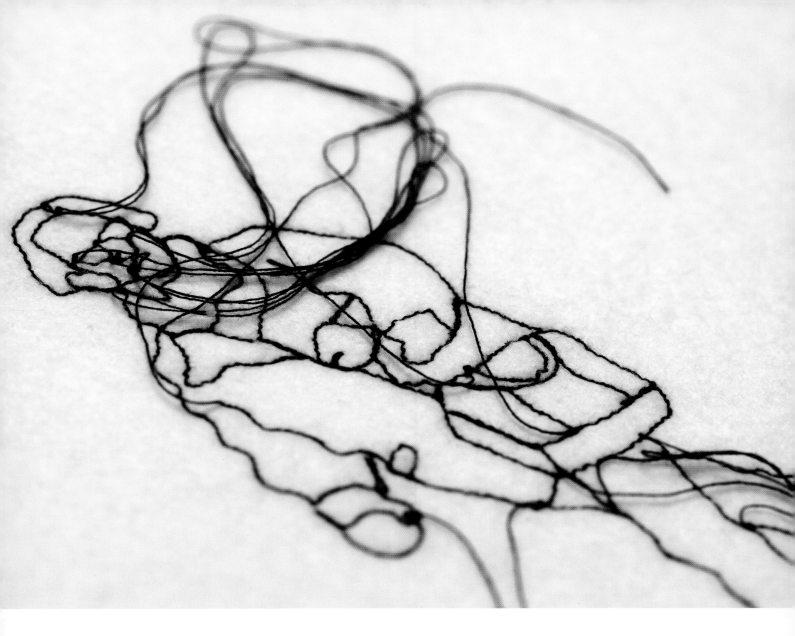

^ A sample showing stitching on felt. Tissue paper was used to transfer the image and also to act as a smoothing element. A hoop was employed to allow free movement.

< Leather is much easier to stitch than you may think, and looks great! Why not try making a purse or a bag from your stitched leather?

such as Stitch 'n' Tear or tissue paper, on the top to prevent the stitching disappearing into the cloth.

Stretchy knits

Stretchy fabrics are tricky to work on, as they won't keep still. Jersey (which most T-shirts are made of) and any knitted cloth will need to be stabilized before you can stitch on it. Use something like Stitch 'n' Tear, an interfacing which you put at the back of the fabric when stitching. It can be torn away on completion. Place both fabric and stabilizer in the hoop. This holds the cloth still and prevents it from dragging as you stitch (see Adding to a Garment, page 117, for an example of working on a T-shirt).

Fabrics with pile

These fabrics include any fluffy, hairy-type cloth, or those with a nap such as velvet or corduroy. With velvets, try putting some Stitch 'n' Tear on the surface before stitching, as this should stop the stitching falling into the nap. However, you may prefer the effect of a sunken stitched line.

With very hairy faux fur, try using a stabilizer, or just tissue paper. Make your drawing on the tissue paper and then lay it over the furry surface. Hoop up fabric and tissue together and stitch as usual. You can then rip away the tissue paper. However, you will need to then play around with the fur and leave some trapped under the stitches, otherwise you will not be able to see the stitched line.

Plastics

Plastic is not a traditional 'fabric', but a variety of non-woven, synthetic, fused-type materials are available, which are great for experimenting with. These are particularly useful if want to make

^ This sample was stitched on silk velvet, which is quite a slithery cloth. The fabric was hooped together with tissue paper.

something waterproof and transparent. Look for fabrics used for shower curtains, for instance. They are very easy to stitch on and can be put in a hoop, depending on thickness. However, they may tear easily, so you need to be careful when stitching a lot of lines next to each other. To make something completely waterproof, you could try stitching on plastic using a fine, synthetic transparent thread. Mind you, the whole thing would be practically invisible!

˅ Figure stitched on red faux fur.

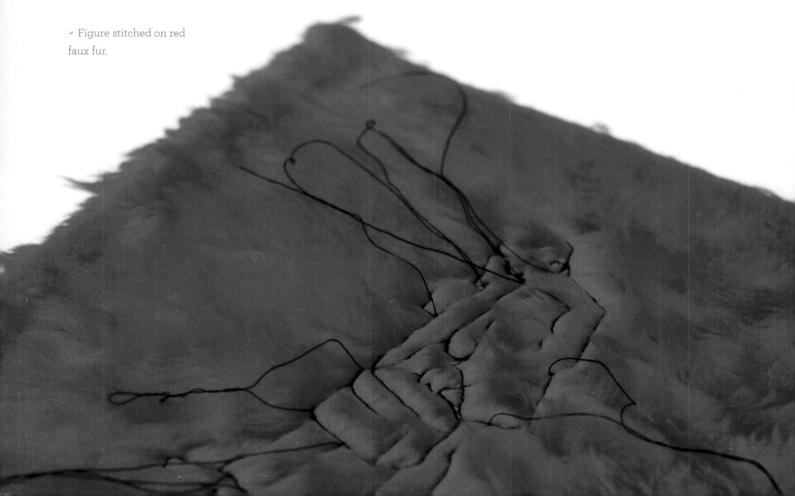

Layers

Now that we have looked at a range of surfaces to stitch on, you can begin to experiment by combining them to form layers, one on top of another, and then stitching. Once done, you can then remove parts of the top layer to reveal a different colour or texture below. Or simply leave them as a sandwich. Try some of the following:

- Fine silk organza on top of a thick felt or wool.
- Plastic on top of fake fur.
- Three layers of a mid-weight cotton, perhaps in different colours, cut away to reveal all the different colours.

˅ Quilted stitched figure. Fine lines of stitching surround the figure, which flattens the background material and allows the figure to stand out.

Quilting

The process of quilting is a follow-on from layering, in that you create a three-layer sandwich of fabrics, with the middle one being a soft wadding. The top and bottom layers are usually a mid-weight cotton. The whole lot can be put in a hoop and free-machined as usual.

Try drawing using a top thread in the same colour as the background cloth. This will allow the padded effect of the quilting to show up well. Experiment also with different types of stitching in order to maximize the padded, puffed-up quality of the quilting; fill in some areas and leave other areas unstitched.

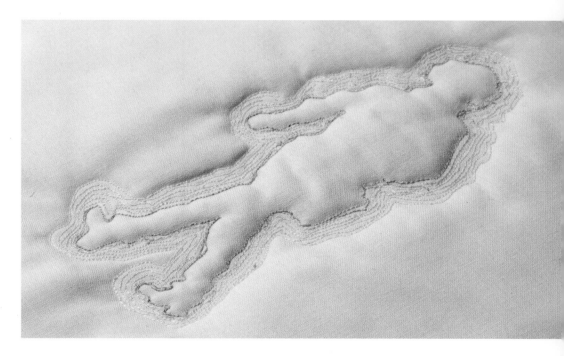

For example, try drawing some small circles and then fill in the area surrounding them. This will flatten the area around the circles and allow the circles to puff up, creating a three-dimensional effect. Experiment with ways to fill in an area: try lines close together or lots of squiggles – each has a different effect.

The sample above was stitched in white on white cotton, using tissue paper to transfer the drawing. I hooped up the three layers of fabric and wadding, and put the tissue paper with the image on top. I then stitched the outline, took off the hoop and removed the tissue paper. Next, I put the hoop back on and stitched the lines around the outside of the figure. If I had left the tissue paper on when doing this, it would have been difficult to get it off.

Stitching without a surface

Using water-soluble substances

We have already looked at using water-soluble fabric or paper as a way of transferring drawings on to another surface. However, these can also be used to create a drawing that is free from its surface, or to create a new fabric made entirely of stitches. There are, in fact, lots of things you can do with water-soluble products once you start experimenting, but in this book we are just going to look at their use for drawing with thread.

ˇ *Study Skins* by Naseem Darbey.

Water-soluble paper

This is just like paper in appearance. It can be printed on using an ink-jet printer, which means that you can print an image on it, place it on the background fabric and stitch around the printed image (you may need a hoop). When done, place the item in water and the paper will magically disappear.

This is quite useful if you have a photograph you wish to draw from and don't want to make marks on the cloth.

SPOTLIGHT: Naseem Darbey

The work of Naseem Darbey provides a good example of the water-soluble technique. She develops the lines of her drawings so that they stand together once the background surface has been removed. This allows her to create pieces that float freely in space and in effect set the drawing free from its surface. Naseem describes the works shown here as hollow drawings. They were made in response to a natural-history collection of taxidermy mounts.

Water-soluble fabric

This is more useful than water-soluble paper for our purposes, and there are a few different types and thicknesses. Some look a bit like clingfilm (or plastic wrap) and others are thicker and slightly less transparent.

As we have already discussed, you can simply use it to transfer a drawing on to cloth, but if you double it up and put it in a hoop, you can stitch on it on its own – like you would a transparent fabric. However, once you wash it, the water-soluble fabric disappears and all you are left with is the thread, which can form a tangled mess! In order to get round this, you need to stitch over each line several times to make it thick enough to stand up on its own. When it comes to washing out the water-soluble fabric, you need to do it carefully: lay the drawing on a tea towel or piece of calico and then gently wet it with a cloth until all the water-soluble substance has gone.

Now you have a drawing in thread that has no surface holding it up, so you need to consider how to hang this work so it can be seen.

Stitched words

The process of drawing with a sewing machine is sometimes referred to as free-machine embroidery. When the feed dogs, which guide the stitching in one direction, are lowered, the stitching can go in any direction you like.

The line of stitching continues for as long as you keep your foot on the pedal and move the hoop around.This kind of freedom of movement lends itself to writing – particularly cursive writing, which does not stop and start.

> This untitled work by Maria Wigley shows how effective stitched words can be once freed from their surface.

Working with scale

Once you have developed a few of your drawings into stitched works, you may want to think about increasing the size of the works you produce. Just because we are using a hoop does not mean that we have to stick within it, so why not go really big? Embroidery is traditionally worked on a small scale, particularly when done by hand, but as we are using a sewing machine it is not too labour-intensive to work at a bigger scale.

Start by drawing what's in front of you on a really large piece of paper. Follow the example of the pieces I made of my shed, described below.

Shed series

The drawings in this series started when I was between projects and wanted to get back to basic drawing. I went into my studio, which is basically a big shed, and just decided to draw it. I laid out a large piece of wallpaper lining paper and started drawing with the intention of filling the sheet, which was about 50 x 65cm (20 x 25½in). I started drawing from the middle of my viewpoint, which was towards the front wall of the shed, and worked outwards until I reached the edge of the paper. I tried to look at what was in front of me and not look at the paper too much. I followed the contours of the shelves and the sewing machine and whatever else was there.

I stitched the resultant drawing on to a large sheet of cotton organdie. I cut this 10cm (4in) bigger all round than my original drawing to allow for putting it in the hoop. Then I traced the drawing on to the cloth. Cotton organdy is transparent but has a slight stiffness to it, a bit like paper. I traced the drawing using a sharp pencil, re-sharpening frequently as the fabric quickly wore down the lead of the pencil.

I inserted the hoop in the top right-hand corner and stitched the lines in black cotton thread; then I re-hooped each section until I had stitched it all.

Once this first piece was complete, I realized that it would be interesting to do another drawing, connected to the first, which moved along the wall and carried on exactly where the first drawing had stopped. This way, a drawing could be made of the entire shed – a sort of panorama of the space that went around the walls and ended back where it had started.

The lines from one drawing follow on into the next. As each drawing is made, the perspective changes and you move your centre of focus; when the drawings are lined up, we get an altered shape. You can see this in the line of the edge of the table.

The interesting thing about working on transparent cloth is that you can hang the drawing in front of the subject, lining up the original with the drawn lines of the stitching.

^ This image shows a section in which we can see the stitched lines of the open door. It is hanging in a space where we can see through the work to the doorway itself: the two line up together, more or less, although the door itself is not visible in the actual space as it is wide open.

^ In this photograph we can see the stitched fabric hanging in front of the area that was drawn. We can see through the fabric from the drawn sewing machine to the actual one. They do not match exactly, but it is interesting to be able to consider the two together in this way.

^ When all four pieces of this series are hung together in a line on a flat wall, they give the viewer a sense of a working space and the paraphernalia and clutter within it.

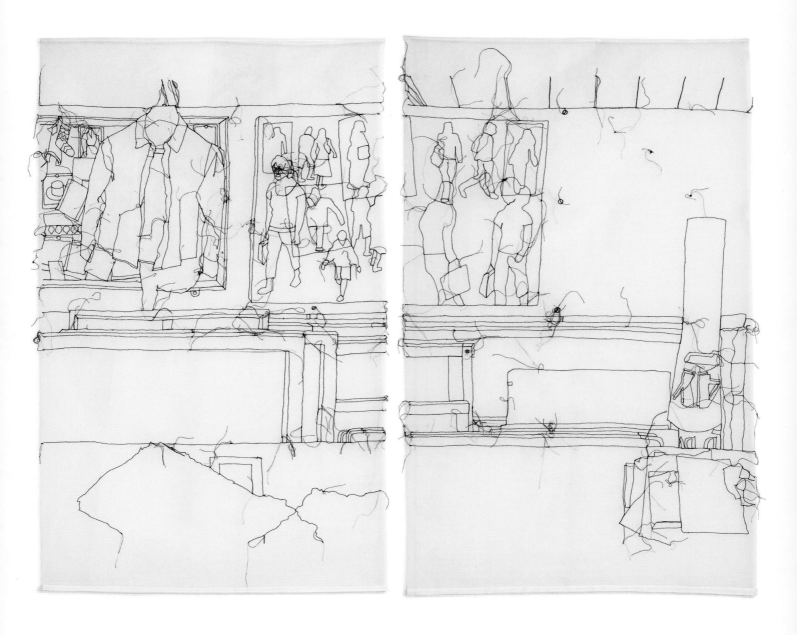

Large-scale figures

The Shed series was worked from drawings made in situ. You may also want to work with your photographs to create a similarly large-scale piece. There are a couple of ways that you can do this with using an overhead projector or a computer.

Overhead projector

Print the photograph on something transparent, such as acetate, place it on the projector and then project it on to a wall. Of course, this is rather old-fashioned technology these days. A rather more up-to-date method would be to have a projector connected to your computer and project a digital photograph on to a wall. Then you can tape a large sheet of paper on the wall and trace around the image.

Computer

Open up the image in whatever photo-editing software you have on your computer – for example Photoshop Elements or Corel PaintShop Pro. Go to the image-size section and alter the size of the image to whatever size you want. If you set the height, the width should adjust accordingly so the whole thing stays in proportion.

Now print out the re-sized image. Remember that you do not need to make a beautiful print as it is only going to be drawn over. It does not matter if you use a low resolution like 72 dpi (dots per inch) – which means a large image will probably be pixelated when printed.

If you have an A4 printer, divide the image into lots of A4-sized squares, print them off and then stick them together to get the full-sized image. Print them in black and white on a low-quality setting to reduce ink usage.

Lay the stuck-together printout on a table, place transparent fabric or tissue paper over it and draw your image. You may want to draw over the print or photocopy first to make certain lines clearer or to make any changes.

Once drawn on to the cloth, hoop up and stitch as usual.

> In my work *Crowd Cloud*, I created a series of life-sized figures. To do this, I first cropped my photograph so I just had the part I needed, then re-sized it to a height of 165cm (5ft 5in), which is an average height for a woman.

< These *Crowd Cloud* images give an idea of the size and scale of the work. The life-sized drawings were grouped together in a space so that viewers could walk around them and we can see through one figure to the others behind it.

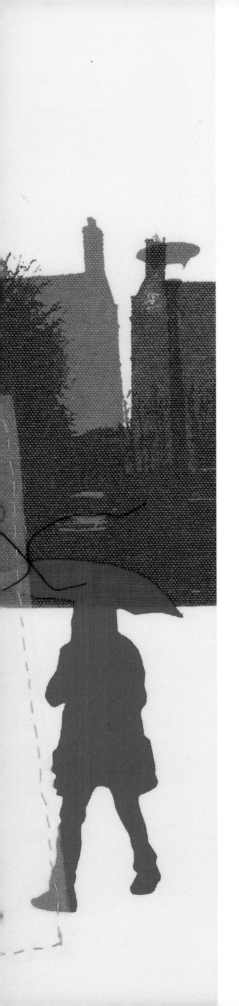

Photography
for stitch

The medium of photography has become a kind of drawing tool used by all sorts of visual artists. Images captured on camera can be so easily manipulated and printed, and then used as a starting point for other media. The first thing to do is to take some pictures. The aim is not to print off beautiful photographs, but to create images to play around with.

Photo journeys

If you are not sure what to take pictures of, why not start out on a photographic journey? Take your camera and leave the house. Set off on a journey to a specific place and as you go, take photographs. If you are using various modes of transport, take photographs from each. The journey can be as long or as short as you like. It could even be your daily commute to work or walk with your dog.

A journey from Rochester to London

This journey started at Rochester Station in Kent and ended at Euston station in Central London. These are just a few of the photographs taken on the day. There were 68 altogether. They were taken with my digital camera, a Canon IXUS with a 12-megapixel sensor.

I wanted to record each stage of my journey and also where I was, so there are pictures of signs as well as of the view from the window. I also included my feet now and then just to show that I was there! You may want to have a focus on certain things that interest you or just go with the flow and photograph whatever takes your fancy. Don't take too many, as there will be a lot to sift through when you get home.

< > Just some of the photographs from my journey.

Editing the photographs

Now you have some photographs to play with, you need a computer to put them on and photo-editing software. There are many photo-editing software programs on the market, but you don't need anything fancy; there may even be one on your computer already. Adobe Photoshop Elements is a good one, as is Corel PaintShop Pro. There are also some free programs available on the Internet.

You need to be able to look at all the photographs you have taken and pull out those that interest you. A good way to do this is to print out a sheet containing thumbnail-sized images of all the photographs you have taken (this is known as a contact sheet). Look at the images and select some that you would like to work from, then start playing with them to get some ideas: cut out bits, draw on the images, stick some in your sketchbook and so on.

Go back to the computer and change the size of the images, print them out again and think about putting images together to create a different kind of picture. Collage elements to create a summation of your journey. As you do this, you can be thinking about which parts would work well as a stitched drawing and which parts could be appliquéd as a fabric shape.

TIP: In order to save ink, use the lowest quality setting on the printer (sometimes called 'fast printing' or 'draft'). The images will be paler than normal, but you are only using them as a design tool to cut out and draw on, they don't need to be perfect.

Once you have worked out a design, transfer it on to cloth (see Transferring a Drawing, page 46).

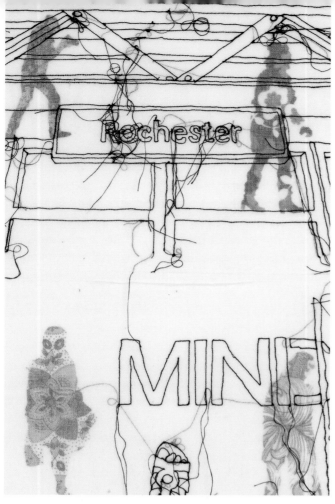

Stitching the Rochester journey

Here is an example of what to do with the photographs from your journey.

After looking at all the pictures from my Rochester journey on a contact sheet, I chose some of them to stitch and decided to put them together horizontally to allow the images to move along as in a journey. However, I then decided that this was perhaps a rather literal interpretation of the idea of a journey, so I resolved to put them together in a vertical line. I wanted the images to work in a way that would suggest a journey on a train, but also link to the people who make that journey every day.

I chose just four pictures to start with and printed them off at A4 size in black and white, setting the printer to 'fast printing' (or 'draft').

I then made a stitch drawing of each image on a piece of transparent organdie, about 10cm (4in) larger than the A4 photograph, with the image placed in the middle so that I could get the hoop to encompass every part of the drawing. I had to move the hoop around in order to stitch the whole thing, starting in one corner and then taking the hoop off and repositioning to complete the rest. Allow 10cm (4in) of cloth around the edge of the drawing to do this. After stitching, I cut around the stitched drawing about 5mm (¼in) from the edge of the stitching.

I used a piece of white cotton canvas to act as a background, cutting out a piece long enough and wide enough for the four A4 size drawings and adding about 10cm (4in) all around to allow me to stretch the piece on a frame.

Before stitching the drawings to the background, I thought about adding some colour. One way of achieving this would be with parts of screenprints, but here I chose to add coloured fabric shapes to represent people, using Bondaweb. I decided to include some figures in this narrative and to make the work about travellers and commuters rather than about my journey. I checked that I had positioned the fabrics in the right place before ironing them on.

Next, I hand-stitched the stitched drawings on top, leaving the loose threads to act as a link from one section to another (of course you may prefer to cut them off).

When the work was completely finished, I stretched it over a frame. (These can be bought cheaply as blank canvases for painting on. Or, if you want a specific size, make your own.)

< > Rochester Journey (right) and close-up details (left) showing fabric figures on the background.

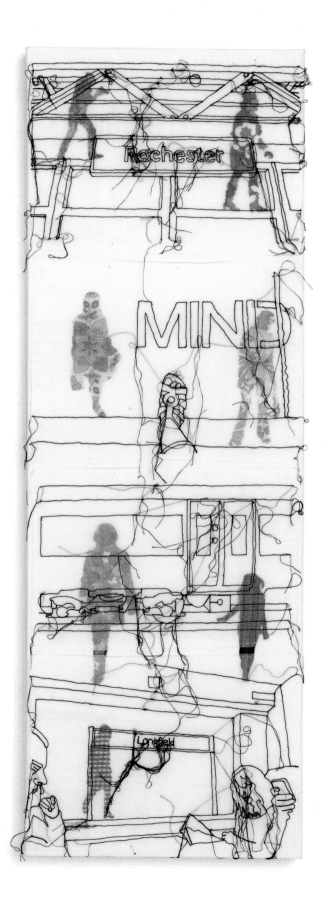

Sequential photography

When you photograph people moving around, you capture a split second, which is gone almost immediately, but if you run a series of still images together, you can create the illusion of movement. This is stop-motion photography, used in animation. We could take a series of stitched drawings and by showing them quickly, one after the other, make that stitched drawing move.

Stitching movement

Using the continuous shooting mode if your camera has it, take a series of photographs of something moving. It could be a person walking along or engaging in some kind of sport, or an animal moving or jumping. Follow the usual process to select images and make a series of stitched drawings (see pages 48–49).

You could then photograph each of your stitched drawings to create an animated film. I have done this with a stitched drawing of a girl walking along. It is a very simple film, consisting of only ten images. The film is called *Girl Walking* and can be seen on my website (see QR link, left).

For the piece below, I photographed a man walking along. I then drew and stitched the images and put them together to move across a length of cloth horizontally, bringing out the man's movements and allowing the viewer's eye to follow him on his journey. The images were overlapped slightly in order to allow the movement to flow from frame to frame.

< Each image of the man was stitched on to the background using a red running stitch. This contrasts with the black and white and also separates the images, giving each one its own boundary and encouraging us to think of each one as a separate frame. The frames make the connection between photography and film, while loose threads add to the sense of movement and urgency.

Using photographs as a surface

As well as using your photographs to draw from, you could also use the actual picture to stitch on. Stitching on photographs adds texture to the glossy photographic surface. The sheen is broken by the loose threads and raised surface of the stitch. The stitched lines can bring a different element of the image to the fore and emphasize previously overlooked aspects.

SPOTLIGHT: Hinke Shreuders

The Dutch artist Hinke Shreuders has employed this technique in her work in an ongoing series of pieces employing fashion photographs in this way. Using black ink and embroidery, Hinke transforms the innocuous images into unsettling vignettes resembling the more narrative fashion editorials of today. Blackened photographs become dense embroidered forests in which the fiercely dressed women appear lost. You can see more of Hinke's work on her website (www.sudsandsoda.com).

If you do not want to ruin your original photographs, scan them and save them digitally. Print off on to fairly thick photographic paper and then stitch on top. Thick paper will stand up to continual stitching and allow you to cover a large area with stitching without the paper falling apart. Another method would be to attach a printed photograph to cloth using Bondaweb. This allows you to stitch quite heavily while still retaining the actual photograph.

> *Works on Paper 31* by Hinke Shreuders. This is one of a series stitched on pages from old fashion magazines from the 1940s and 1950s. You can see the rough edges where the page has been ripped from the magazine. The addition of the stitched lines changes the focus of the images. In this work, Hinke has used a lot of stitching and almost obliterates the original photograph.

A note about copyright

Artists often appropriate images to use in their work, particularly images from newspapers and magazines, in order to make a point. However, using images that belong to other people without their permission can lead to copyright infringement and you could be taken to court or fined.

It is always best to use your own photographs – this is the only way to avoid any copyright issues. If you must use other people's images, ask permission first. If you are not making the images for commercial gain, you may be able to get permission from the publisher. If it is not possible to ask permission, you need to change the image substantially in order to use it. It could be argued that by drawing from an image and then stitching it, you have changed it enough. However, this is debatable, so to avoid this issue, use your own photographs!

Adding colour

Colour can be brought into stitched drawings in all sorts of ways – by stitching on a background of coloured or printed fabric, by using different coloured threads for the top thread and the lower thread, by creating blocks of colour (filling in areas with scribbly stitching), by adding appliquéd fabrics, or by including painted or printed sections.

Coloured background

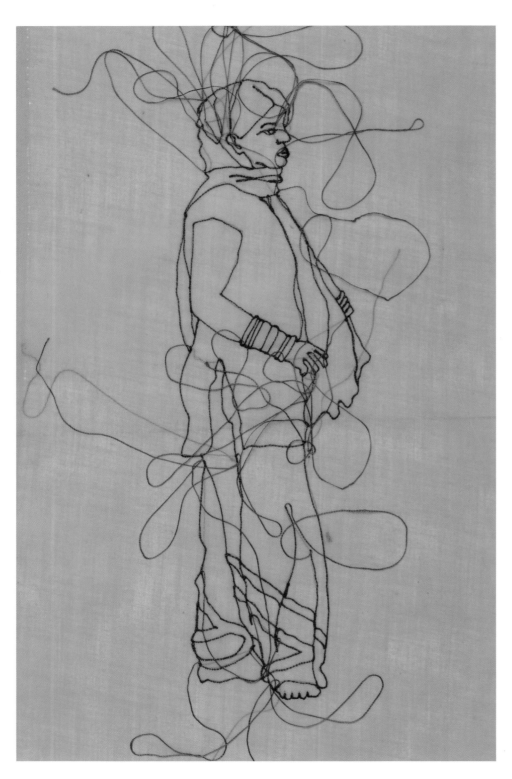

The cloth you stitch a drawing on can be any colour you like but be careful that the colour of the thread you use is strong enough to be visible on top of the background.

The background fabric is the base for all the elements of a design, and may be stretched across a frame or made into a bag or cushions, for example, so make sure it is strong enough for your purposes.

< *Lady at a Sikh Temple* by Rosie James, stitched in pink thread on lime-green cotton. The pink thread stands out well against the green background, showing off the stitching to good effect.

Patterned background

How about using a patterned background fabric? In *Maidstone Mela* (above), I used a piece of red-and-white patterned fabric as the base. This was a piece of batik cloth, made by drawing in wax on the fabric and then dyeing it red. Batik originated in Indonesia and is used in other countries such as Malaysia, Singapore and India. The work depicts people at an event that celebrates the different cultures living in an area, and the batik fabric sums up the multicultural aspect of the work.

The batik cloth was used as a background and the figures added on top. In order to make sure the figures stood out from the background, I appliquéd a piece of white cotton behind the stitched outlines.

^ *Maidstone Mela* by Rosie James. Working on a patterned background fabric can be tricky. Here I used black stitching for contrast and appliquéd white fabric behind the figures to help them stand out.

Different coloured threads

A sewing machine uses two sets of thread: the top thread and the thread in the bobbin. If the threads' tension is perfect, you should not be able to see the bottom thread on the surface of the cloth. However, you can alter the tension on the top thread slightly so that the bottom thread gets pulled to the surface, and then both colours will be visible and can give a nice dotty effect (see pages 36–39). This image shows a red bobbin thread and a black top thread. The top tension was tightened to bring the red from the bottom to the surface.

> Stitched sample using a black top thread and red bobbin thread on white cotton polyester. The tight top-thread tension brings the red thread up to the top.

Loose threads

You can also add colour by leaving a lot of loose threads in a different colour to the stitched line.

SPOTLIGHT: Nike Schröder

This technique can be seen very expressively in the work of Nike Schröder. Nike has developed the use of loose threads and often adds more to play around with colour creatively.

˅ > *Transition 12* (right) and *Transition 13* (below) by Nike Schröder. In these works the colour seems to drip from the canvas like paint as the colours blend into one another.

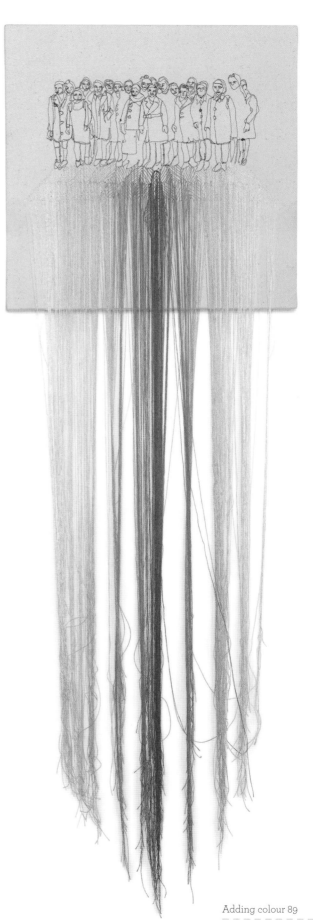

Blocks of colour

So far, we have looked at drawing distinct lines with the sewing machine. But you can also use the back and forth movement of the machine to fill areas with solid colour.

There are various specialist machine-embroidery threads made of rayon and constructed to glide easily through the eye of the needle. These are quite shiny and produce beautiful, shimmering colour when built up over a surface. You can use the same colour for the top thread and in the bobbin, or you can use a transparent thread in the bobbin so that all the colour remains on the top of the fabric, and not on the underside.

Once you have stitched an outline for the area, thread the machine with the colour for filling in, re-hoop the drawing and stitch over and over in the space you wish to fill using a straight stitch. If you want a bit of texture, use a zigzag stitch.

˅ Rosemary Milner used hand-embroidered stitches to fill in the colours in this piece, called *Meadow Hares*. For more information about Rosemary's work, see page 115.

ᵛ In this piece by Leigh Bowser, which is called *Anatomical Heart*, Leigh has used very bold colours to get a visually striking effect, strengthened by the use of black line.

Appliqué

You can bring in coloured or printed fabric elements to work as a block of colour, either within the lines of a drawing or as a separate thing altogether. Using the technique of appliqué – the attachment of one piece of cloth to another using stitches or Bondaweb – coloured fabrics can be applied to a background cloth. You can then stitch into them or layer other fabrics on top.

Gillian Bates uses plain fabrics to add blocks of colour to her stitched drawings. She places the colours very sparingly, allowing the drawing to dominate. The artworks are very reminiscent of pen and watercolour, in that the colours have a subtle pastel tone to them.

In my own work, I like to use appliquéd fabrics to add extra people and figures as a separate element. Gillian Bates uses coloured fabrics to fill in areas between the drawn lines, but an extra dimension can be brought in by adding fabrics away from these lines.

< *Harbour Site* by Gillian Bates. Gillian has used a few colourful elements in the form of appliquéd plain fabrics to enhance her sketchy style of stitch drawing. The resulting image has a distinctive, eye-catching and cheerful style.

Consider the kinds of fabric you use and what they could add to the connections between the drawn line and coloured elements, then use appropriate fabrics to tell your story.

In the work shown left, called *Stripey Strollers*, I have used pieces of shirting fabrics which were cast offs from a Savile Row tailors. These fabrics are worn mostly by men working in office jobs and so can be used to convey the sense of hustle and rush felt in our busy working lives.

It can be interesting also to use fabrics which reflect the place depicted in your drawing. The example below, called *Indian Ladies at the Gurdwara*, uses Indian fabrics in a piece depicting women at a major temple in Delhi.

< *Stripey Strollers* by Rosie James. The fabric used – shirt cast offs from a Savile Row tailor – are appropriate to the office-worker subject matter.

< *Indian Ladies at the Gurdwara* by Rosie James provides colour with appliquéd Indian fabrics appropriate to the subject.

Using Bondaweb for appliqué

Bondaweb is a double-sided fusible webbing made by Vlieseline/Vilene. It is also known as transfer adhesive. It is used to bond fabrics together and is ideal for appliqué projects as it can be used to make a cut-out shape into an iron-on motif. Bondaweb comes on a paper backing.

To use it, trace (or draw) the shape of the motif on to the paper backing, then cut it out roughly. Place it on the back of the fabric to be used for the motif, webbing-side (rough side) down. Iron the paper for five seconds (no steam) for the surfaces to bond. Now cut out the motif accurately.

˅ Using Bondaweb for appliqué is quick and easy, but note that you get a mirror image of your drawing (to counteract this, see instructions shown right)

Peel off the backing paper from the motif and place it, coated-side down, where you wish to appliqué it to the background fabric. Cover with a cloth or baking parchment and press it, on a two-star to three-star heat setting. Leave flat while it cools for 1–2 minutes.

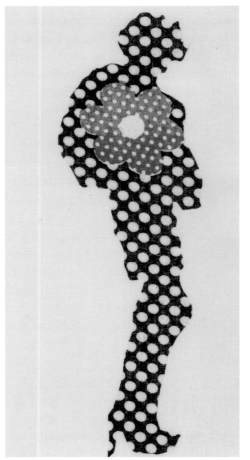

Appliquéing a photograph of a figure

1 Print out a photograph (at the desired size) of the figure you want to appliqué. Use the lowest-quality setting on the printer – 'fast printing' or 'draft' – to conserve ink; you only need to be able to see the outline.

2 Place the Bondaweb over the image with the backing paper uppermost and trace around the outline of the image. Cut roughly around the shape – do not cut along your pencil lines just yet!

3 Iron this on to the back of your chosen appliqué fabric. Make sure it has completely adhered before using a small pair of sharp scissors to cut carefully along the drawn lines of the figure.

4 Peel off the backing paper and iron the figure motif on to the front of the background fabric. Make sure it has completely adhered to the cloth. Leave it to cool before moving it.

Using this method, the figure will be reversed; in order to achieve a figure that is the right way round, you can either print it out as a reversed image to start with, or you can flip the backing paper over after tracing.

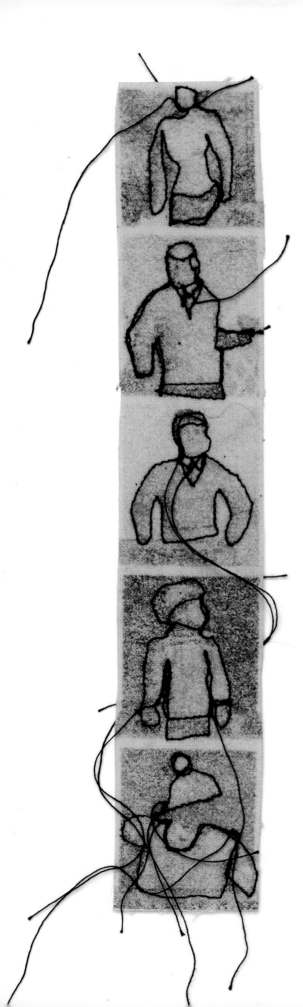

Printed sections

You can also add colour by printing sections of fabric to add to your work. Try using different surfaces and experimenting with putting fabrics through an ink-jet printer.

If you want printed fabrics to be washable, you must treat the fabric first using a liquid product such as Bubble Jet Set (see Suppliers, page 125). Soak the fabric following the packet instructions and leave to dry before putting the fabric through your printer. However, if you do not plan to wash your artwork, this won't be necessary.

Attach the cloth to some paper in order to guide it through the printer. Make sure that you use a thin, flat fabric with no fraying edges. Loose threads can damage a printer, so don't try this if you have a very expensive printer!

Put a strip of double-sided tape across the top of the paper and attach the fabric, then place it in the printer, inserting the taped edge first, and click Print. Alternatively, iron cloth onto freezer paper to stabilize it before putting it through the printer.

You can also print on Bondaweb: simply cut out an A4-sized sheet, including both webbing and backing paper, and feed it through the printer as usual, printing on the webbing.

Iron the print, webbing-side down, on to some white cotton. The result will be a slightly fuzzy image.

You can then stitch into the print, as on the printed Bondaweb sample shown left. Remove the backing sheet and discard it before stitching. The print will be slightly sticky at first, but this dries over time.

< Small sample showing
stitching onto calico, which was
first printed using Bondaweb
put through an ink-jet printer.

Basic screen-printing

I use screen-printing in some of my work to add colour, but also to set the scene of the piece. Most of my work focuses on groups of people and crowds, and usually I like to keep the location out of the work and look just at the people. However, sometimes it can add to the narrative of a work to bring in elements of the location.

For instance, in one early work, *Pergamon Lecture* (not shown), I was interested in people sitting on some steps and listening intently to a man who was standing before them. The screen-printed strip at the top of the piece depicts part of the Pergamon Altar in the Pergamon Museum in Berlin. This work shows a variety of colour: the stitched figures have been done in blue, and the steps are hand-stitched in orange. The screen-print is a stone colour.

A follow-up piece takes the colour even further. In *Pergamon Audio* (shown right) we see people sitting on the same steps looking at the same Pergamon Altar, but instead of listening to a person talking they are all wearing headphones to listen to the audio commentary. In this work, much brighter colours were used, with the figures stitched in red and the screen-print made in black and blue on coloured panels – a reference to Andy Warhol's famous brightly coloured screen-prints of Marilyn Monroe. This time, the steps were hand-stitched in a natural grey. Notice how some of the figures overlap the screen-printed section. This helps to integrate the two distinct sections of the piece.

> *Pergamon Audio*, by Rosie James. Machine-stitched in red with hand stitching in grey. The background has been screen-printed on linen with silk organza. The process for screen printing is described on the following pages.

Equipment and materials

You may like to experiment with this medium to add a further dimension to your work. Let's start by trying some simple screenprints using cut paper stencils. This is easy to do with some quite basic equipment and can be very effective. All you need is:

- A screen
- A squeegee
- Textile printing ink
- Thin paper such as photocopy paper

Make a screen

A screen is just a wooden box frame with some fine mesh fabric stretched over it. You can buy ready-made screens, but it is much cheaper to make your own.

1 Take four lengths of wood and glue them together with wood glue, then staple them at the corners with a staple gun.
2 Stretch some polyester voile across the frame. This is cheap to buy from furnishing-fabric shops, as it is mostly used for making net curtains. Staple it all around the edge of the frame, as shown left. Make sure it is as tight as possible.

If you are in a hurry and don't have time to make a frame, you could use an old picture frame with the glass and backing removed, or a large embroidery hoop. Simply put the polyester voile in the hoop and tighten it up as much as possible. Of course, this is a round screen instead of a rectangular one, so make sure it's big enough for the image you plan to print.

Squeegee and ink

A squeegee (far left) is used to force the ink through the screen. You can buy this from an art shop; however, improvised tools are often just as good. A grouting tool (left) is ideal for small prints, and much cheaper than a squeegee. An old credit card could even be used for printing a very small image.

Textile printing inks are available in many different types, and all are good; just make sure a potential ink is water-based and suitable for use on your particular type of cloth.

Printing table

You need to create a suitable surface on which to print. Cover an old table with a discarded blanket, then cover that with some plastic sheeting and staple both to the table. Then completely cover everything in a sheet of medium-weight calico: this is the backing cloth.

The blanket creates a surface with a bit of give in it, so that you can push the squeegee down into the mesh of the screen. The plastic will protect the blanket. The backing cloth soaks up any excess ink that goes through the fabric you are printing on and prevents it from bouncing back to the print to create a double print.

Printing

We are going to use cut paper shapes to create a printed image: when ink is pushed through the screen, the shapes will block the ink and a blank space in the shape of the paper cut out will appear. You could use some of the shaped pieces of Bondaweb backing paper left over from making appliqués. I always keep mine: I have loads of them!

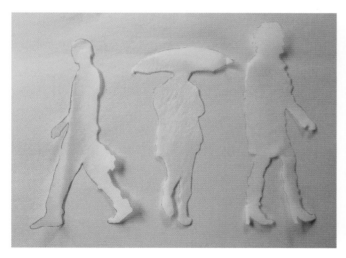

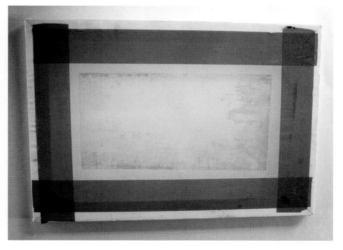

1 Lay the shapes (I'm using figures in this example) on the fabric you wish to print on. Tape or pin the fabric to the backing cloth.

2 Mask the edges of the screen in order to create a shape around the figures: stick packaging tape on the outside of the screen.

3 Next, place the screen face down over the fabric, with the figures positioned within the tape frame on the screen.

4 Put some ink along the top edge of the screen. Hold the squeegee at 45 degrees and drag it along the mesh from one edge to the other. Apply some pressure and make sure you scrape the sharp edge of the squeegee along. This is known as a pull. Two pulls will probably be enough for a good print on thin cotton, so turn the squeegee and drag it back up the mesh to where you started.

5 Lift the screen from the fabric to reveal the print. The paper figures will now be stuck to the mesh and you can print as many times as you like until the paper deteriorates.

6 If you want to print another colour, wash the screen and start again. I printed on top of the green print with blue ink, just shifting the position of the screen slightly. I did not wash the screen between printings as I was happy for the blue and the green to blend together a little. However, I dried the green print with a hairdryer before printing over it.

7 Most textile printing inks are set by heat. Once the print is dry, you will need to iron it for a minute in order to fix it to the cloth and make it washable (follow the manufacturer's instructions).

8 You can now stitch into your print. Why not add some appliquéd figures in a patterned, colour-coordinated fabric to create a busy little group?

Using stitched drawings to print with

Once you have a made a screen, the possibilities for printing are endless. You can use all kinds of things to place between the screen and the cloth. The only proviso is that they must be as thin as paper – anything thicker will result in thick, blobby prints. Leaves, grass and lace can work well, as do threads.

You can also use stitched drawings to print with. The lines of the stitching will block the ink in the same way as paper shapes. You need to stitch on thin, transparent fabric for this to work.

1   Place the stitched fabric on the fabric you are going to print on, put a blank screen on top and then print over it as described in the previous exercise. Try two pulls. Lift off the screen and then remove the stitched fabric.
2   There will be a white line where the stitched line has blocked the ink. This can be quite a good effect for creating contrasting lines and marks within one piece.

< Sample showing the resulting print when screen printing over a piece of stitched organza. The print is shown on the left, and the original stitched piece on the right.

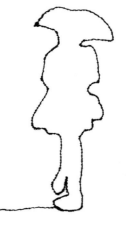

Subjects and presentation

What are you going to draw and how will you present it? There is so much to inspire you, but where do you start?

Subject matter

So far, we have been looking at drawing and photographing the things and people around us. We have simply been recording what we see and then considering how to record that in stitch. But how do you narrow down the plethora of subjects? You will be drawn to record particular things that interest you. Look at what you have chosen to draw or photograph and consider the connections between the various things; pull out the common threads and then start to think about how you can explore these ideas further. Here are some ways to go about it:

1   Collect images. Cut images from newspapers and magazines, but mostly look online. For example, in my own work I have become fascinated by crowds and collect images of different kinds of crowd. This can be done online, using a web-based system such as Pinterest or Tumblr. Pinterest is particularly good for creating boards of images and for searching for interesting images. Another useful site is Flickr, which is a photograph-sharing website.
2   Read books. Research your chosen fascination through words as well as visual imagery. Look for books or articles relating to your subject. Look also at poetry and fictional prose.
3   Use a dictionary or thesaurus. If you are stuck with an idea and unsure how to develop it, open up a thesaurus or look at an online version and search for words with a similar meaning. Write them down and consider the differences and connections between them. Maybe one will take you off in a different direction. Choose one of the words and consider how you would illustrate that word.
4   Listen to music.
5   Watch films.
6   Read newspapers.
7   Go to the theatre.
8   Visit a museum.
9   Visit an art exhibition.
10 Collect stuff (tickets, leaflets, flyers and so on). Never throw anything away!

Gather all your collected images, words and notes. Now sort them, arrange them, think about them, and note down any ideas that come to you for a new project. You won't have time to do them all, but keep the list going. Then if you are stuck later on, you can revisit some of your old ideas.

Putting ideas together

Try putting together images and words as a way of thinking, perhaps with no clear idea of the end result. Experiment with mixing different media.

SPOTLIGHT: Lisa Solomon

Lisa Solomon has a way of putting together images and different media and marks. Her work makes lovely juxtapositions between the thread and the pencil line, using imagery that seems quite surreal but which does have a story behind it.

While researching her Japanese heritage, Lisa discovered that the Japanese developed incendiary devices called Fu-Gos or balloon bombs during the Second World War. They launched 9,300 of these balloons to be carried on the jet streams. While mostly ineffective, some did land in the US. Pastor Archie Mitchell, his wife Elsie and five children from his Sunday School set out to picnic in Gearhart Mountain forest near Bly, Oregon. The children discovered a balloon bomb and it exploded, killing all the children and Mrs Mitchell. Lisa's piece, *May 5, 1945*, is a dedication of sorts to them. The map pinpoints the place (with a red map pin) where it happened. The six empty balloons represent the six people who were lost. Lisa rendered the balloon with machine stitching (alluding to quilting: safety, warmth), but leaving the thread tails long to invoke thoughts of loss and destruction.

The image tells a story, but in a way that allows the viewer to connect the individual elements.

˅ *May 5, 1945* by Lisa Solomon juxtaposes a map, balloons and thread to tell a story.

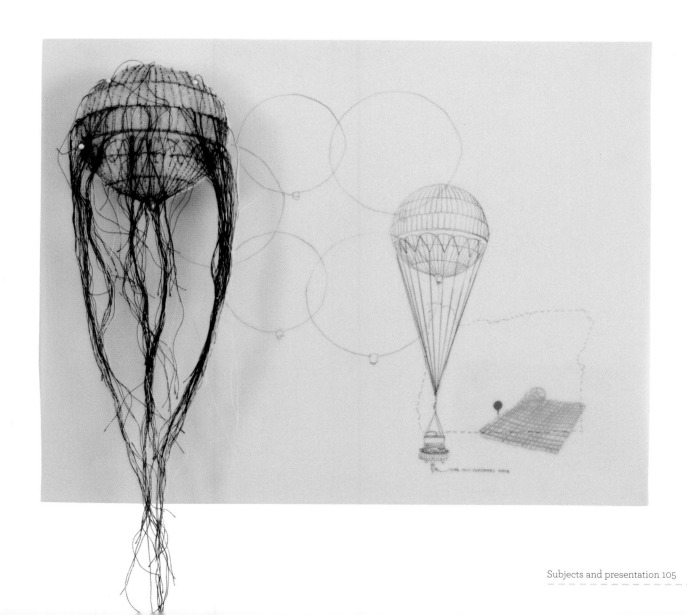

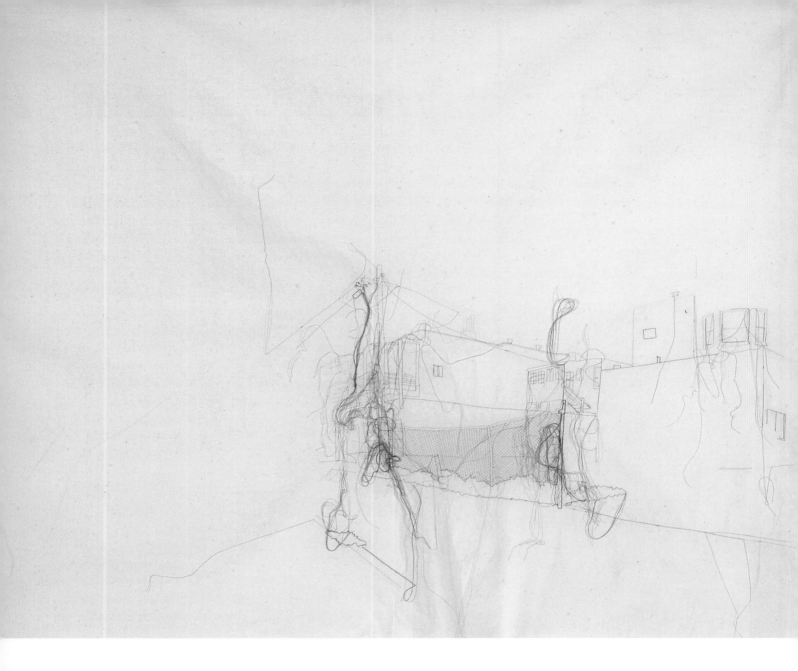

SPOTLIGHT: Tucker Schwarz

Tucker Schwarz is an artist who uses stitch to create landscapes. She chooses quite pale colours and minimal lines to draw buildings and streets in a wide, empty landscape. The example above shows an empty urban landscape. There is a quiet, contemplative quality to the work.

^ *Well I Suppose That* by Tucker Schwarz. The pale and minimal lines are achieved using thread on muslin.

SPOTLIGHT: Rachel Coleman

Rachel Coleman uses a wide range of different media in her work to create a lively, almost noisy quality that is the polar opposite of Tucker Schwarz's work.

∧ <∨ *New York 6* (above), *Flying Seagull* (left) and *Contemporary Nativities* (below) by Rachel Coleman.

Making a statement

You could use your work to get an idea across that you feel strongly about: consider stitch as a way to make a point. It can be just as effective as paintings and sculpture. The use of stitch can make a powerful image even more resonant and emotive. We are familiar with fabric: we wear it, we sleep in it, and we have a strong connection to it. The homemade, domestic qualities of fabric, combined with stitch, draw us to it and make it a powerful tool with which to express ourselves.

SPOTLIGHT: Leigh Bowser

Leigh Bowser used her stitching skills to develop the Blood Bag Project, which was to raise awareness of a rare blood condition suffered by her niece. The resulting imagery is powerful yet simple, and I think the fact that it is stitched makes it even more evocative and moving.

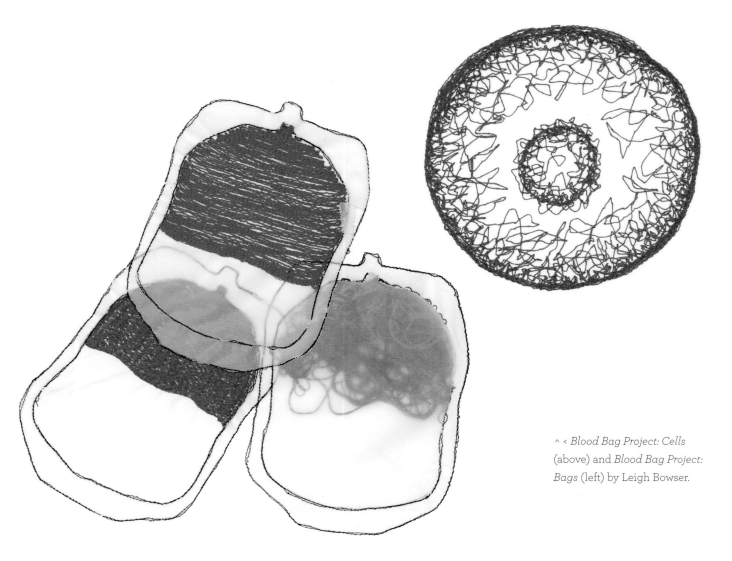

^ < Blood Bag Project: Cells (above) and *Blood Bag Project: Bags* (left) by Leigh Bowser.

< *Necklace* by Sophie Strong. Stitched drawings depicting a variety of images taken from newspapers and put together to make a neckpiece.

SPOTLIGHT: Sophie Strong

Sophie Strong trained as a sculptor and now uses stitch as she feels it has a sculptural element to it. Her subject matter is based on humanity and extreme emotional circumstances. Sophie says:

'So many of my embroideries are of countries of conflict or oppressive government. The images are drawing based, from photography used in newspapers. Without these photographers, these embroideries would not exist.'

The use of stitch in these images can make a powerful image even more powerful and emotional. Stitching and cloth can transform an impersonal image into something with which we have a strong personal connection.

Presenting your work

What are you going to do with your completed stitch drawings? Here are some ideas for final presentations that you may wish to consider when thinking about your next project.

Stretching over a frame

I present my own work in this way quite a lot. You can buy a ready-made frame in the form of a pre-stretched canvas for artists. As you are not going to paint on it, you don't need to spend a lot of money on a good surface. Simply stretch your work over the canvas and frame and staple it on the back. The piece of canvas adds strength and also means that the back of the work cannot be seen.

These stretched canvases come in a wide variety of sizes, but be careful when using large ones. Inexpensive canvases are made of cheap wood, which distorts easily. Sometimes it is worth paying a bit more or to get them made professionally to your exact measurements. You can also make your own, using your own choice of wood (see page 98), or use an old picture frame to stretch your work over.

The back of a framed work, showing how to staple the canvas to the frame.

^ Stitched birds on a vintage
doily on a handkerchief
by Rosemary Milner. Here
the hoop frame gives the
impression that the work has
just been finished and reminds
us of the traditional work that
has gone into it.

Displaying in a hoop

This is a very simple way of displaying your work. Leave the work in the hoop and
hang it on the wall! That's it, basically, but you will need to tidy up the edges of
the cloth so they are not visible. This can be done by trimming the edges or by
stitching across the back of the frame to hold the fabric edges together. Consider
using a decorative frame to hang the work in, or paint a simple wooden one in a
colour matching the work. Red or black works well as a strong contrasting colour.

In this piece, Rosemary Milner has framed her work in a hoop, leaving the edges
of the beautiful handkerchief it has been stitched on for us to see.

Using a picture-frame mount

This is a slightly unconventional way of using a conventional picture frame with a glass front. The work ends up in a frame but the stitching is not squashed behind glass.

In the examples shown here, I stitched a drawing on transparent cloth (in this case cotton organdy). Taking a piece of patterned cloth (this could also be patterned paper), I cut the shape of the drawing from the middle of it and attached the remaining cloth to some card. I inserted the cloth plus card into a frame, put the glass on top, then placed the cotton organdy on top of this. I used double-sided tape to attach the organdy to the glass along the top and bottom edges (this wasn't visible once in the frame).

The loose threads remain on top and are not trapped by the glass. The glass in the middle creates a distance between the two elements, helping the stitching to stand out and adding a kind of three-dimensionality.

< ˅ Detail of two small works which used old photographs as their inspiration. The layers can be seen clearly with the patterned background behind.

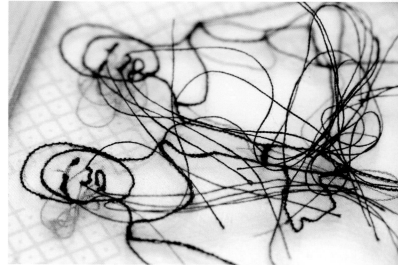

Hanging loose from a rod

Sometimes it is not advisable to stretch your work, for example, if you have used a delicate fabric that may rip if stretched, or if it is too thick to do so. Perhaps you want the work to hang freely as a wall hanging. Quilters often use the rod method of display as quilts are too thick to stretch and have a finished edge that needs to be on show.

I use this method when working with large pieces on silk organza. For the work *Crowd Cloud*, I created life-sized drawings of figures that were intended to be hung freely in a space and not against a wall. For this purpose I used transparent acrylic rods stitched into a tube along the top of the fabric. I wanted the hanging method to be as invisible as possible.

Creating a product

Drawings made with a sewing machine can be put to use on all sorts of products. You can make bags, brooches, clothes, cushions, curtains, ties, scarves – the possibilities are endless. You could start with easy things such as cloth bags and cushions. Just bear in mind that if you like to leave loose threads, these can get caught up and pull so it may be a good idea to cut them off.

˅ Three of the *Crowd Cloud* figures, which were hung from transparent rods (for more on the *Crowd Cloud*, see pages 70–73)

Adding to an existing item

Rather than making a product from scratch, why not simply add your stitched drawing to an existing item, such as a garment or tablecloth?

<Stitched drawing of a stag on an antique doily by Rosemary Milner. Working on an existing item provides ready-made confines and can provide ideas for themes. It can be a wonderful method of rcycling too.

SPOTLIGHT: Rosemary Milner

Rosemary Milner uses existing items to great effect by adding her own contemporary stitch work to antique stitched pieces. In the work shown here, Rosemary has stitched on a vintage doily. It allows the viewer to make connections between the beautiful handmade edging of the doily and the stitched illustration within it, and consider the different hands that have worked on this piece over the years. Rosemary has turned it from a useful home item into a piece of artwork. As she says:

I use the sewing machine more as a drawing medium within my embroidery pieces, as it is a good way of creating texture in a quick, fluid motion. I combine this with freehand embroidery techniques such as appliqué and a mixture of stitches. This combination of traditional and modern techniques is a running theme throughout my collections and enhances the narrative element of my pieces. The concept behind the embroidery stems from a love of the British countryside and historical tales from the Victorian era. Growing up next to the North York Moors has also fuelled the inspiration behind my work and defined me as a designer.

Display

Something like a stitched doily can be quite difficult to display. It may be best kept as a decorative item on a flat surface. However, if you wish to hang it on a wall, it can be mounted and framed. I suggest that you get this done professionally. If you want to try it yourself, attach the work to a piece of mounting board, possibly with double-sided tape and some discreet stitches. Put it in a frame behind glass, but leave sufficient space between the glass and the piece so that the work is not squashed.

Adding to a garment

Try stitch drawing on a garment. When you wear it, everyone will be able to see and admire your handiwork.

In the example shown right, I used a white shirt to work on. The intention was to use the shirt as a blank canvas and not to create something wearable (however, you could wear the end result). I wanted to use the shirt as a kind of sketchbook to try out ideas and combinations to see what worked and what didn't. I planned a mixture of screen-print and stitch. The screen-printed imagery was taken from haberdashery items, bits of thread, pattern pieces, sewing instructions and also some screen-printed drawings of people out shopping.

On top of the screen-printed imagery I added stitched drawings of figures. These drawings were transferred using the water-soluble fabric method (see page 47), and the result is an interesting mix of drawings in stitch and print.

If you do not want to wear the end result, you can display it on a tailor's dummy (look out for a nice vintage one) or simply hang it on a coat hanger placed on a hook on the wall.

You can add stitched drawings to any kind of garment: skirts are good in that they have large areas of flat fabric and so are easy to work on. T-shirts are fun, too, but you need to be careful as the fabric is stretchy. In the example shown left, I traced the drawing on to silk organza, positioned it on the T-shirt and then put the two together in a hoop. This meant that the silk stabilized the stretchy jersey fabric of the T-shirt. When stitching was complete, I cut around the excess silk up to the edge of the stitching. I used small, sharp embroidery scissors and was careful not to cut the black thread of the stitching.

If you do not want to use an extra fabric on top of a T-shirt, you can use a stabilizer on the wrong side of the shirt fabric. A product such as Stitch 'n' Tear is a good one to use: draw the image on it in reverse and then position it on the wrong side of the T-shirt. Put it in the hoop and stitch your drawing, working on the wrong side of the shirt. When complete, tear away the stabilizer. (A few bits may remain in the embroidery, which is why you put it on the back. If you look at manufactured garments with embroidered elements, you will see the stabilizer fabric on the reverse of the embroidery.)

^ *Sew What?* by Rosie James, screen printed and stitched white cotton shirt. A personalised garment like this could be worn or displayed as art.

< *St Dunstan* by Rosie James, stitched in black thread on silk organza and a white cotton T-shirt.

Making a book

A book is an interesting way of displaying your work. You can stand it up on a shelf, or flick through it like a traditional book. Books are traditionally made of paper, but an artist's book can be made of absolutely anything. The examples here are made of cloth and don't stand up, but they can be flicked through just as you would a normal book.

In this book (shown right and below) I created an accordion-style fold-out section of silk organza. On this I stitched some walking figures. The folds were stitched right along the edge in order to sharpen and emphasize them, and also to allow the book to fall back into place when folded up. The cover has two appliquéd figures cut from black silk organza.

< ˅ A cloth book, made with a white cotton canvas cover featuring appliquéd black fabric figures. The accordian-style pages, made from silk organza, unfold when you open it up. This simple style of fabric book is great for showing off your work, especially panoramic scenes or motion sequence.

Cloth books

It can be fun to create cloth books. Cloth books may be somewhat floppier than the paper variety, but can be picked up and 'read' or displayed on a wall in a frame. They are also particularly useful as a way of displaying samples that you want to refer to.

If you create stitched drawings on a series of pieces of cloth of the same size, put them all together and stitch up the middle, you will have a cloth book. You may need to neaten the edges to prevent fraying, and this can be done with an overlocker, zigzag stitch, or simply by using pinking shears.

Here are some examples of books I have made as a way of trying out different techniques or ideas. Bringing these together as a book means that I can easily show them to people or just to refer to them when revisiting an idea. I like to think of them as cloth sketchbooks.

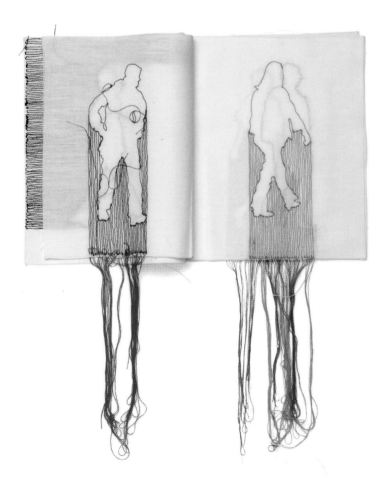

^ > When you open up this book, the coloured drawings are revealed.

In the book shown opposite, I wanted to experiment with lines and colour. I developed some stitched drawings with silhouettes of figures and lines of colour, leaving the threads to cascade out of the bottom of the book. The cover shows my intentions, with the outline of a figure and stitched lines emanating from it. However, we can also see the coloured threads hanging from the bottom edge of the book, hinting at what's inside.

The book shown opposite is about 30cm (12in) square. You may want to make something much smaller, especially when making samples. The book shown right and below is only 15cm (6in) square – this is just big enough to allow you to play around with imagery.

> For this book, I made a screen-printed cover using a blank screen and an image cut from a fashion magazine. Place the image on top of your cloth, put your blank screen on top and print (for more information about screenprinting, see page 96). Inside the book the stitched drawings also feature images from fashion magazines.

Conclusion

'[Drawing is] the formation of a line by drawing some tracing instrument from point to point of a surface; representation by lines; delineation as distinguished from painting ... the arrangement of lines which determine form.'
The Shorter Oxford Dictionary

'Drawing is like making an expressive gesture with the advantage of permanence.'
Henri Matisse (1869–1954)

'Until we can insert a USB into our ear and download our thoughts, drawing remains the best way of getting visual information on to the page. I draw as a collagist, juxtaposing images and styles of mark-making from many sources. The world I draw is the interior landscape of my personal obsessions and of cultures I have absorbed and adapted, from Latvian folk art to Japanese screens. I lasso thoughts with a pen.'
Grayson Perry (born 1960)

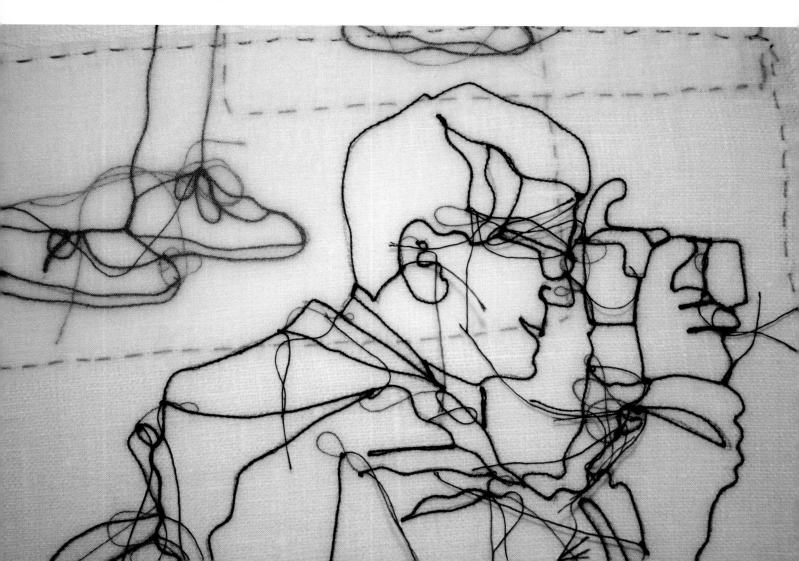

Featured artists

Gillian Bates
Images of seaside towns like Brighton. Line and colour.
www.gillian-bates.com

Leigh Bowser
Blood Bags campaign, machine-stitched portraiture.
www.leighlalovesyou.tumblr.com

Cathy Cullis
Figurative stitched drawings and mixed-media art.
www.cathycullis.blogspot.co.uk

Lisa Solomon
Mixed media and stitch with loose threads on paper.
www.lisasolomon.com

Rachel Coleman
Mixed-media stitched drawings, whimsical animals and more.
www.rachelcolemandesigns.co.uk

Nike Schroeder
Fine-art stitched figurative drawings with loose threads.
www.nikeschroeder.com

Tucker Schwarz
Landscapes and architectural stitched drawings with loose threads.
www.gregorylindgallery.com/artists/schwarz

Rosemary Milner
Stitched drawings of animals and birds on vintage fabrics.
www.rosemary-milner.co.uk

Sophie Strong
Dynamic stitched images taken from newspapers.
www.sophiestrong.co.uk

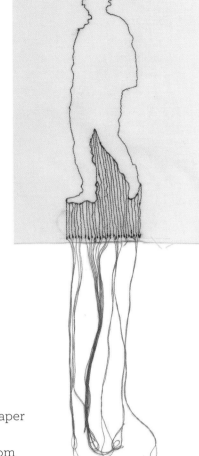

Hinke Shreuders
Stitched pieces on paper and photographs.
www.sudsandsoda.com

Mags James
Paintings and illustrations.
www.illustratormags.blogspot.co.uk

Naseem Darbey
Work on water-soluble fabric.
www.naseemdarbey.com

Maria Wigley
Pieces featuring stitched text.
www.mariawigley.co.uk

Further reading

Whole Cloth by Mildred Constantine and Laurel
    Reuter, Monacelli Press, 1997

Drawn to Stitch by Gwen Hedley, Batsford, 2010

Machine Stitch Perspectives by Alice Kettle and Jane
    McKeating, A&C Black, 2010

Fashion Designers' Sketchbooks Two by Hywell
    Davies, Laurence King, 2013

Push Stitchery by Jamie Chalmers, Lark Crafts, 2011

Contemporary Textiles by Janis Jefferies and Bradley
    Quinn, Black Dog Publishing, 2008

By Hand: The Use of Craft in Contemporary Art
    by Shu Hunh and Joseph Magliaro, Princeton
    Architectural Press, 2007

The Subversive Stitch by Rozsika Parker, I. B. Tauris,
    2012

The Art of Looking Sideways by Alan Fletcher,
    Phaidon Press, 2001

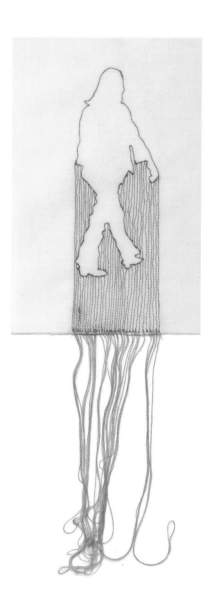

Suppliers

Whaleys Ltd
www.whaleys-bradford.ltd.uk
For plain white cottons, silks and many more ready
for printing or stitching on. Also Bondaweb (transfer
adhesive) by the metre.

George Weil Fibrecrafts
www.georgeweil.com
They sell everything you need for a huge variety
of textile techniques and other crafts.

Jeffay Furniture Ltd
www.artiststretcherbars.co.uk
This is where I get all my stretcher frames made
especially for the large pieces.

The Plastic Shop
www.theplasticshop.co.uk
They sell acrylic rods of all lengths and widths. I use
these for hanging pieces made with transparent cloth,
when I don't want the hanging system to be visible.

Crafty Computer Paper
www.craftycomputerpaper.co.uk
All kinds of papers and fabrics, which you can
put through your inkjet printer. And then transfer
onto cloth.

Barnyards
www.barnyarns.co.uk
They sell all sorts of gorgeous threads suitable
for machine embroidery.

Jaycotts
www.jaycotts.co.uk
Sewing machines and needles, feet etc and a wide
variety of haberdashery, sewing patterns and more.

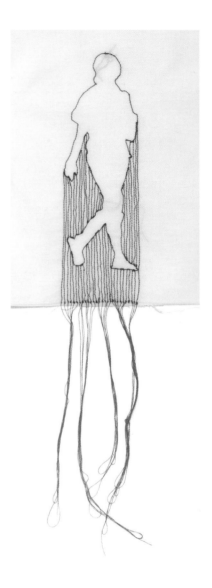

Index

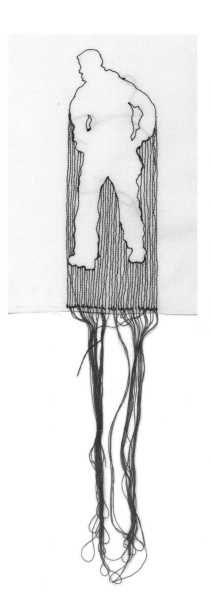

Rosie James is a textile artist with an art background. She runs workshops on her stitch-drawing techniques throughout England, and exhibits widely.

Also available from Batsford:

Text in Textile Art by Sara Impey
9781849940429

Stitch and Structure by Jean Draper
9781849941211

Connecting Design to Stitch by Sandra Meech
9781849940245

To receive regular email updates on forthcoming Pavilion titles, email update@pavilionbooks.com with your area of interest in the subject field.

Visit **www.pavilionbooks.com** for a full list of our available titles and **www.batsford.com** for more from Batsford.